Luther's Gospel

Luther's Gospel

Reimagining the World

Graham Tomlin

Bloomsbury T&T Clark
An imprint of Bloomsbury Publishing Plc

B L O O M S B U R Y
LONDON • OXFORD • NEW YORK • NEW DELHI • SYDNEY

Bloomsbury T&T Clark

An imprint of Bloomsbury Publishing Plc

50 Bedford Square	175 Fifth Avenue
London	New York
WC1B 3DP	NY 10010
UK	USA

www.bloomsbury.com

First published 2017

British Library Cataloguing-in-Publication Data
A catalogue record for this book is available from the British Library.

ISBN: PB: 978-0-5676-7739-6
HB: 978-0-5676-7740-2
ePUB: 978-0-5676-7741-9
ePDF: 978-0-5676-7742-6

Cover image © Engraving by G. Spangenberg in Scherr, 'Germania' /
Mary Evans Picture Library

Typeset by Newgen Knowledge Works (P) Ltd., Chennai, India

For Nathanael

ACKNOWLEDGMENTS

The Editors, Publishers and Author ('Graham Tomlin') gratefully acknowledge the permission granted to reprint the Author's following material in these publications:

Chapter 1: Luther and His Gospel
Tomlin, G., 2004. 'Shapers of Protestantism: Martin Luther'. *The Blackwell Companion to Protestantism*. Blackwell Publishing Ltd, pp. 40–52.
This chapter has been significantly revised since its original publication.

Chapter 2: Luther on Bible Translation
Tomlin, G., 2013. 'Luther's Approach to Bible Translation and the KJV'. *The King James Version at 400, Assessing Its Genius as Bible Translation and Its Literary Influence*. The Society of Biblical Literature, pp. 125–140.

Chapter 4: Luther on the Death of Christ
Tomlin, G., 1998. 'The Medieval Origins of Luther's Theology of the Cross'. *Archiv für Reformationsgeschichte*. Gütersloher Verlagshaus, pp. 22–40.

Chapter 5: Luther on Pilgrimage
Tomlin, G., 2004. 'Protestants and Pilgrimage'. *Explorations in a Christian Theology of Pilgramage*. Ashgate Publishing Ltd, pp. 110–125.

CONTENTS

PREFACE

Luther's life and thought have occupied my mind for many years. He is frequently provocative, usually perceptive, often wrong, frustratingly stubborn, yet always interesting. Unlike many an early modern theologian, he is rarely dull to read. Over the centuries, Luther has been read in many different ways and it will be fascinating to see if and how the five hundredth anniversary of the beginning of the Reformation in 2017 will produce another reading of the reformer, or enable him to speak again to concerns of an age very different from his.

It is relatively easy to co-opt Luther into whatever agenda we happen to want him to back, on the basis of a few carefully chosen citations. Luther is one of the most quotable theologians, even if some of the quotes that do the rounds have little basis in anything he actually said! At least in part because he wrote so much, it is not difficult hastily to claim him as an ally, if the proper historical work has not been done. On the other hand, historical work on Luther can simply leave him as an oddity, a voice that spoke to the concerns of sixteenth-century Europe, but is of little value today, an age in which people's questions seem very different from those of Luther's contemporaries.

This book is written from the perspective that on the one hand we need to do proper historical research, as with any other figure in theological history, and read Luther closely in the context of late medieval theology and society, to do justice to his thought. Like any other thinker, he makes little sense without an understanding of his historical context and the ideas and events he was reacting to in his own time. There are no shortcuts beyond close, careful reading of the texts and relating them to their historical context. Luther was, as we all are, a person of his time. Theology can never be abstracted from its historical context, and is always shaped by it. There is no expression of theology that is not historically conditioned, and so we need to do the hard work of placing ourselves as much as possible in his world to understand him well. Yet Christian faith in general, and Luther's theology in particular, has at its heart the incarnation, in which the eternal Word took flesh at a particular moment. Truth speaks in historical clothes – it roots itself in time, yet transcends it nonetheless. The best theology, though based in history, is never confined by it. Luther is therefore not just a sixteenth-century voice. He is one of those theologians who somehow continues to speak to the concerns of ages very different from his own. Each centenary of the Reformation found new, or reread old, aspects of his thought to inform and shape Christian life in those ages, and this time it will no doubt be the same.

This book argues that there is a simple insight at the heart of Luther's thought that dominated everything else: the idea that we are justified, or put right, not by any internal quality we may possess, but by something outside ourselves altogether – the goodness or righteousness of Christ. Our identity, or our sense of worth, is therefore not self-defined or self-constructed, but is given to us by God in Christ, a realization that relieves us of the great burden of having to construct our own rickety sense of self in competition with others. This insight is then worked through in Luther's subsequent thought into a whole series of other areas of life and faith – issues such as prayer, marriage, pilgrimage or freedom, to give some examples. The book traces how this insight affects a kind of reimagining or redefinition of life.

It starts with three chapters analysing Luther's understanding of the gospel, rooted in his reading of the Scriptures. It proceeds with three more chapters that examine how his understanding of the gospel led him to a transformation of late medieval patterns of Christian life, in particular, meditation on the passion of Christ, the practice of pilgrimage, and personal prayer. The last three chapters look at his practical and theological teaching on three topics of medieval and modern interest – sex and marriage, the devil, and freedom.

As I look back on thirty years of reading and studying Luther, I am conscious of a debt of thanks to many. I remain grateful to Alister McGrath, whose lectures on Luther in Oxford in 1985 first stimulated my interest in him. I am also thankful to the many students at Wycliffe Hall, Oxford University and St Mellitus College whom I have taught on Luther and whose questions and discussions (and sometimes, to their surprise, even whose essays!) have made me discover and think through new aspects of his thought and their implications. I am also grateful to other colleagues who have helped my thinking on Luther in discussion, and by pointing me to reading other aspects of related theology, particularly Chris Tilling, Sean Doherty, Lincoln Harvey and Peter Walker. Others played an important role in the material in this book by extending invitations to lecture or write on these topics, including Richard Burridge, Craig Bartholomew, Tory Baucum and Pete Greig. Others helped at various stages in the process of writing the book, including Anna Turton from T&T Clark, and Heidi Cormell.

I am particularly grateful to Alden McCray who stepped in at short notice to do a good deal of editing and formatting of the book. I'm grateful for his detailed and painstaking work at hunting down references, formatting footnotes and adding his growing wisdom in Reformation studies to enhance the project.

Lastly, I need to record my debt to my wonderful family, who must have often felt that Luther was a quasi member of our household over the past thirty years. Sam (who shares a birthday with the great man – not planned – I assure you!) and Sian, our children, have come, in their own way, to appreciate Luther in their own studies, but mostly I am grateful to Janet, my wife, who has cheerfully endured and maybe occasionally even enjoyed the many conversations about Luther in our home over the years. Like Luther, I am grateful to have enjoyed the blessing of a good wife, and a loving family over many years. The book is dedicated to the newest member of our family, with the prayer that he will come to know and love the Saviour whom Luther knew and trusted.

Graham Tomlin
Feast of the Conversion of St Paul, January 2017

PART A

Luther and His Gospel

1

Luther and His Gospel

During the last millennium, the world changed radically. Marco Polo and Christopher Columbus opened up new continents, William Shakespeare and Michelangelo produced some of the most sublime pieces of art, and Napoleon Bonaparte and Adolf Hitler changed the political face of their centuries. Yet a good argument can be made that one medieval monk outstripped them all in historical significance.

Martin Luther and the Reformation he triggered have made a huge impact not just in Europe, but also in North America, Australia and the rest of the world. Around 800 million people worldwide belong to the various 'Protestant' denominations, none of which would exist without the events surrounding Luther's protest against aspects of Catholic Christianity five hundred years ago. Protestantism has shaped a whole new way of life for people across the Western world and beyond, which has coloured their approaches to God, work, politics, leisure, family and, in fact, to almost every aspect of human life. It played a seminal role in the early development and continuing self-image of the United States, in the emergence of democracy and economic and religious freedoms in Europe, and was one of the key movements ushering in the changes from the medieval to the modern world. Luther cannot claim credit or blame for the whole of what eventually became Protestantism, but as one who played a critical role in the emergence of a new church and a new way of life for millions of people, the influence of his actions and beliefs on the past five hundred years has been incalculable. The modern world can barely be understood without them.

Martin Luther was not the author, but became the accidental instigator of the Protestant Reformation through his famous protest about the abuse of Indulgences in 1517. He remains one of the Christian church's most influential theologians, who gave his name (unwillingly, it must be said) to a whole denomination and initiated a new way of Christian living, praying and believing across Europe.

At the start of this book, which offers a variety of reflections on aspects of Luther's influence and thinking, this first chapter seeks not only to introduce the Reformer to those for whom his life and actions are less familiar, but also to ask the more important question of what made him stand out: what was his understanding of the Christian gospel, and what made it so remarkable that we are still talking about it five centuries later?

Luther's Story

Born Martinus Luder in 1483, in Eisleben, Germany,[1] his youth was relatively peripatetic, due to his father's involvement in the mining industry, as a part-owner of a mining company. Martin spent most of his childhood in Mansfeld, and went on to matriculate at the prestigious University of Erfurt in 1501. A dramatic, even traumatic experience in a thunderstorm in 1505 led to his entry into the monastery of the Augustinian Order in the same city to begin life as a friar. This event was a vital stage in a process of searching for personal salvation characteristic of many in this age of spiritual and theological uncertainty. However vivid the experience, it did not indicate a termination of his study, but merely a refocusing away from his father's preferred pathway of a career in the law or the civil service of the empire, towards the study of theology. Luther's time in the monastery was deeply formational for his future life and spirituality, both positively and negatively, yet he soon found himself led in a more academic direction, under the supervision and guidance of his superior in the Augustinian Order, Johannes von Staupitz. He was ordained a priest in 1507, and subsequently transferred formally to the new University of Wittenberg in 1511

---

[1]He later changed his name to Luther, following the custom of many Humanists at the time who chose significant names – 'Luther' echoed 'Eleutheria', the Greek word for freedom.

to succeed Staupitz as professor in biblical studies, a post he held until he died.

During his time in Erfurt and the early years in Wittenberg, Luther began to question important aspects of the theology and church practice he had been taught from his youth. The nature and timing of this are both complex and disputed. Sometime in the period between 1514 and 1520, Luther's own theological understanding, particularly of the doctrine of salvation, was transformed. Much debate has taken place over dating the 'Reformation Breakthrough', though it took place most probably not in one single moment of insight, but in a series of stages – the best image is probably that of Heiko Oberman who refers to a series of breakthroughs between 1513 and 1519,[2] like waves on a beach, each one bringing the tide further in. Whenever it happened, it led to a decisive break from the theology and piety of his contemporaries, and eventually from the papal church itself.

In the autumn of 1517, Luther became concerned about the abuse of Indulgences, certificates issued by the church that remitted punishments imposed as part of the medieval penitential system. Indulgences had begun to be applied not only to the church's earthly requirements, but also to punishments to be endured in purgatory. They could also be applied to deceased relations who were believed to be suffering the torments of purgatory. An Indulgence backed by Archbishop Albrecht of Mainz, and preached near Wittenberg by the renowned Indulgence-seller Johann Tetzel, drew Luther's fire. His basic complaint was that these certificates offered a form of cheap grace, and 'false assurance', encouraging people to trust in letters of Indulgence rather than God's mercy, inveigling them to avoid the true and painful contrition that alone rendered the sinner receptive to God's grace.

Luther's protest took the form of a letter to the archbishop, enclosing ninety-five theses, which were effectively a challenge to academic debate. These were subsequently passed on to friends who rapidly printed and distributed them, and the document came to be interpreted as an attack on both clear conciliar teaching and papal authority. In this period from late 1517 to 1520, in dispute with papal theologians such as Cardinal Cajetan, Sylvester Prierias

---

[2]H. A. Oberman, *Man between God and the Devil* (New Haven: Yale, 1989), pp. 165–6.

and Johannes Eck, the implications of Luther's developing theology were slowly drawn out. Particularly in his debates with Eck, the similarities between his ideas and those of the executed Bohemian heretic Jan Hus became obvious, as was the clear water between his own teaching and that of recent Councils on Indulgences (especially the Council of Constance in 1415) and papal decretals. The result was formal excommunication in January 1521, followed by an appearance before the emperor Charles V at the Diet at Worms later the same year after which Luther was placed under the imperial ban, an edict that was never fully implemented in Luther's lifetime.

Much of these debates focused around the role of Scripture in Christian life and theology. Luther's focus on 'Scripture alone' as the final authority for Christian life and thought emerged from two distinct but related aspects of his early development. During the course of his controversy with papal theologians before his excommunication, Luther appears to have been surprised by their refusal to tackle him on the grounds he wanted to argue, namely, the teaching of the Bible. It is easy to see why they refused to do so – to argue point by point with an obscure German monk over the interpretation of Scripture would itself concede the ground they wanted to protect – the ultimate authority of the Church, vested in the pope and councils, to interpret Scripture, rather than any individual Christian, however well theologically trained and qualified. As a result, all Luther encountered was the repeated charge that his ideas were opposed to both papal and conciliar teaching, and therefore to be condemned. While he began the Indulgence controversy with a somewhat naïve expectation that Scripture, pope, councils and canon law would be seen to be in agreement, these controversies soon drove a firm wedge between Luther's reading of Scripture and these other authorities. The failure, or refusal of his opponents to answer him with Scripture compelled him towards asserting the authority of Scripture over against these other authorities, rather than complementary with them.[3]

The other force that shaped his emerging doctrine of Scripture was experiential. Luther's experience of Christian life from early times, and subsequently in the monastery, was marked by what he later called '*Anfechtung*', the experience of doubt and despair,

---

[3]For a good discussion of this process, see S. H. Hendrix, *Luther and the Papacy: Stages in a Reformation Conflict* (Philadelphia: Fortress Press, 1981).

especially focused on the question of whether God looked on him with favour or condemnation. His theological discoveries did not banish these experiences, they simply gave him the means to deal with them. Such experiences were particularly acute during the controversy with the papacy, and produced a consequent need for reassurance that could be trusted. In extremis, Luther found that a human word such as papal teaching, the pronouncement of a council or the word of eminent theological authorities could not give him the solid ground he needed. Only a word from God in Scripture presented itself as an unyielding foundation on which he could stand firm while the storms of conflict or conscience raged around him. As a result, his famous stand before the emperor to whom he was summoned at the Diet of Worms in 1521 took the form of an appeal to Scripture: he was 'bound by the Scriptures I have quoted and my conscience is captive to the Word of God'.[4]

This break with Rome did not, however, lead to a seamless development into new forms of Christian life. For the rest of his life, Luther found himself embroiled in further disputes, particularly with other reformers within the evangelical movement itself. These debates were to divide the Reformation movement profoundly. Some centred around political theology, over the tactics of the 'Peasants Revolt' of 1525, and his subsequent development of his idea of the 'two kingdoms' in response to the peasants' use of violence to achieve their aims, and the confusion between political and ecclesiastical power in the late medieval church. Others centred around the interpretation of the sacraments, the role of the law in Christian life, monastic vows, education and numerous other issues, many of which are examined in this book.

For the remainder of his life, until his death in 1546, Luther was based in Wittenberg. He spent many hours and words working on the reformation of the church in Saxony, his home region, and on a project that was always among the closest to his own heart: the translation of the Bible from the original languages into a colloquial and accessible German.

For Luther, the church needed not just moral or spiritual reform, a renewed effort to uproot scandals and malpractice from the church, or a deepened and more serious commitment to prayer and

---

[4]Martin Luther, *Luther's Works*, 55 vols (St Louis and Philadelphia: Concordia and Fortress Press, 1955), 32.112. Hereafter *LW*.

the spiritual life – it also needed theological renewal. He came to believe that the church in recent times had lost its way, and had allowed certain ideas to become mainstream, which effectively led away from the heart of the gospel. Strengthened by his strong sense of calling, through his academic training, to be a 'doctor of the church', he believed that God was restoring the gospel to the heart of the church in such a dramatic way that this was perhaps a kind of precursor to the end times. There was always a strongly apocalyptic dimension to Luther's thought: that the crisis of his own time was not just a merely historical event, but also an eschatological one, a time when the powers of evil were doing their worst to silence the gospel, and the powers of God were enabling the good news to sound out all over again.

Luther's Gospel

If the church's primary need was theological renewal, the key question has to be: what was at the heart of Luther's understanding of the gospel? The question can be answered in two ways, which need to be closely related to each other. One answer is historical, the second concerns the contemporary relevance of Luther's theology for today.

First, the historical question: What was it about Luther's theology that marked him out from other theologians of his time? This was a time of great theological uncertainty, with faculties in universities divided between older Scholastic methods, the new radical tones of Nominalist philosophy and theology, and the methods and values of Humanist study. Many theologians were arguing in different directions in the early sixteenth century, so what made Luther different? Why did he start a Reformation rather than any other?

Viewed purely historically, the origins of the Reformation were more accidental than deliberate. It is clear that in 1517 Luther did not intend to start a Reformation in any organized sense when he started the Indulgence affair. Erwin Iserloh has argued fairly persuasively that the event most people envisage as launching the Reformation on 31 October 1517, the posting of the 95 Theses on the door of the Castle Church in Wittenberg, probably never happened.[5] Luther never refers to that event, claiming that he only posted a letter to his Archbishop Albrecht of Mainz on that date, enclosing his theses, as a way of raising his concerns about Indulgences, as others had before him. Luther always claimed that he gave the authorities time to respond, only going public with his protest when they failed to do so. If he did post the theses publicly on that day as well, it would mean that he lied in claiming that he gave them time to reply, going public on the same day in which he wrote privately to the church authorities. When we add in the fact that the story of the posting comes from Philip Melanchthon, who was not in Wittenberg at the time, the likelihood grows that this was an accretion to the original event, a legend that has become confused in the telling. More significantly, it emphasizes the sense that Luther had no intention of starting a revolution in October 1517. He did not go public with the protest at the start, but privately raised this issue with his bishop, and it was only when he received no satisfactory reply, and the theses began to circulate more widely, leading to his being taken to task for his ideas by delegates sent from the papal church to argue him into submission, that he began to diverge radically from conventional ways of thinking and arguing about theology. The debates with papal theologians such as Prierias, Cajetan, Eck and others only served to radicalize his theology, first by Cajetan's refusal to argue with him on the basis of Scripture, and second by Eck's masterful manoeuvring him into agreement with the heretic Jan Hus over sacramental theology and soteriology.

If the historical origins of the Reformation were somewhat accidental, we are still left with the question of what were the theological ideas that eventually caused the rift. What was the key idea or ideas that marked out Luther from all other early sixteenth-century theologians?

A central feature of Luther's theology was, of course, his renewed understanding of the 'righteousness of God' (*iustitia dei*). The best-known description of this change was in his famous 'autobiographical fragment' of 1545, where he recalls the beginning of the Indulgence controversy. In his early theological career, as he pondered the scriptural use and meaning of the phrase '*iustitia dei*',

---

[5]E. Iserloh, *The Theses Were Not Posted* (London: Geoffrey Chapman, 1968).

particularly its occurrence in Romans 1:17. Luther described this as his turn from a view, common within systematic works of theology at the time, of this as 'active righteousness', or God's own righteousness by which he actively condemns sinners. Instead, he began to understand it as 'passive righteousness', a righteousness that God works in, or gives to sinners, and that is received by faith. Hence God's *iustitia* became for Luther not demand but gift – not so much 'justice' but 'righteousness'. Acceptance of sinners by God as truly righteous came at the start of, and as the essential precondition for, the grateful living of Christian life, rather than a goal to be achieved at the end of it. Christians were not partly righteous and partly sinful, with the Christian life as the slow process, to be completed in purgatory, whereby such sin as remained could be removed, until final acceptance by God was achieved. Instead, Christians were, in Luther's well-known phrase, *simul iustus et peccator* – 'at the same time righteous and sinful': fully righteous by virtue of the righteousness of Christ received by faith, despite and yet simultaneous with the real presence of sin.

Faith is therefore hearing the promise of God that he justifies the ungodly (Romans 5:6), and simply believing it. Faith therefore includes both a positive and a negative aspect. Positively, it lays hold of and clings tightly to the Word of promise, which offers forgiveness and grace; negatively, it refuses to try to earn any kind of personal merit before God on the basis of which a claim might be made for his favour. Faith resolves to take God at his word and therefore eschews the attempt to impress God with works: it is by definition the opposite of 'works' – passive receptiveness of grace, not active cooperation with it.

Behind this focus on justification lies a significant shift in the understanding of anthropology and soteriology. All previous versions of scholastic medieval soteriology suggested to varying degrees that the granting of salvation required the acquisition of merit, with the help of God's grace, so that a person became righteous within themselves, and it was on the basis of this internal righteousness, once complete, that justification was bestowed. In various ways, medieval theologians from Peter Lombard to Thomas Aquinas to Gabriel Biel (based, it has to be said, on aspects of Augustine's teaching) all suggested that salvation was granted on the basis of internal factors – merit, or a righteousness, goodness or holiness that belonged to the person who performs works deserving of such merit, although assisted in various ways by grace – therein lay the key differences between the various types of late medieval soteriology. Salvation was granted on the basis of something the individual comes to possess within – a righteousness that cannot be generated without the help of grace (no medieval theologian believed in justification by works in that sense), but that is truly one's own. Salvation depended, essentially, on becoming good.

Luther, however, insisted that the righteousness that justifies a Christian is not his or her own internal righteousness at all, however much assisted by divine grace, but is, instead, an external or strange righteousness (*iustitia externa* or *aliena*), an 'alien righteousness, that is the righteousness of another, instilled from without. This is the righteousness of Christ by which he justifies through faith.'[6]

Justification comes through reception of a righteousness that is precisely not one's own. It is Christ's righteousness, accepted by faith alone. The practice of good works flows from justification, but does not in any way contribute to it. Salvation does not depend on the performance of meritorious works, even those performed with the assistance of grace. Justification was granted solely on the basis of the merits of Christ, imputed to the believer through faith alone.

This debate was focused around the issue of merit. The spiritual life, according to most medieval theology and spirituality, centred around the acquisition of merit through good or pious actions. There were subtleties over the kind of merit acquired, whether condign merit – merit in the strict sense of the word – or congruous merit – merit accruing to works not strictly speaking meritorious, but deemed to be so by divine mercy. Either way, the fact is that most late medieval theologians worked with the idea of merit as something accrued by the individual over time, as he or she cooperates with grace, growing towards holiness.

Luther began to challenge this from his early days. Strangely perhaps, his fire was never focused on any one particular medieval theologian. If there was one great villain of the piece, it all stemmed from medieval theology's dependence on Aristotle. Luther's *Disputatio contra scholasticam theologiam* of 1517, even more radical and significant theologically than the 95 Theses of the same year, was a direct challenge to Aristotle's ethical teaching,

---

[6]*LW* 31.297.

which had been taken over into most forms of scholastic theology. The whole piece, with its stress on the bondage of the will, and the necessity of grace for the performance of any good work, opposes the idea that salvation can be based on anything within the sinner. Such a teaching sought righteousness in virtues nurtured and possessed by the human agent. As Aristotle always said, we become righteous by doing righteous deeds. Instead, for Luther, love for God leads not to becoming more virtuous, but more aware of one's own sinfulness, a process that takes place through suffering, not the acquisition of merits. Luther stands apart from what he saw as the effectively Pelagian theology of the *via moderna*, theologians such as Gabriel Biel, who thought God would reward with condign merit works done without the help of grace. He even distances himself from Thomists who denied this, and held to God's initiative in giving grace to enable the primary act of turning to God. For Luther, the distinctions did not matter. Both adherents of the *via antiqua* (such as Duns Scotus or Thomas Aquinas) or the *via moderna* (such as William of Ockham, Pierre d'Ailly or Gabriel Biel) looked to human righteousness rather than Christ's, a righteousness that was internal, not external.

As we shall see later in this book, for Luther, 'external righteousness', the righteousness of Christ received by faith, is the key to a true 'internal righteousness'. The alien righteousness of Christ releases the self from anxiety about one's own salvation in order to give oneself in true goodness to the neighbour in acts that are truly other-directed, rather than subtly done for one's own salvation. Luther genuinely believed in spiritual formation, but thought it had nothing to do with justification: 'This righteousness goes on to complete the first, for it ever strives to do away with the old Adam and to destroy the body of sin. Therefore it hates itself and loves its neighbour; it does not seek its own good, but that of another, and in this its whole way of living consists. For in that it hates itself and does not seek its own, it crucifies the flesh. Because it seeks the good of another, it works love. Thus in each sphere it does God's will, living soberly with self, justly with neighbour, devoutly toward God.'[7]

This distinction on the grounds on which justification takes place, whether on the basis of a person's own formation in holiness

---

[7] *LW* 31.300.

over time (even beyond life itself into purgatory) or on the basis of the alien holiness and goodness of Christ, received by faith, lies at the heart of Luther's theological revolution. It is the one thing that distinguished him from all other late medieval theologians. It also lies at the heart of most of his subsequent theological development and his debates with contemporary figures.

Christology

This view of justification led to an increasing focus on Christ as God's gift. For Luther, the Christian holds on to the gift of Christ as the eternal pledge of God's favour and grace, over against any voice of accusation or experience of abandonment that might suggest God is unmerciful. God's act in Christ becoming human for us pledges him to us once and for all, and is the foundation of Christian faith and peace: 'If you see that God is so kindly disposed toward you that he even gives his own Son for you, then your heart in turn must grow sweet and disposed toward God. And in this way your confidence must grow out of pure good will and love – God's toward you, and yours toward God.'[8]

To hold to Christ as God's gift and pledge to us required a Christology that held Christ's divine and human natures closely together in unity: 'In Christ there is a divine and a human nature, and these two natures in one person, so that they are joined together like no other thing, and yet so that the humanity is not divinity, nor the divinity humanity, because that distinction in no way hinders but rather confirms the union.'[9] The two natures were not separate entities coexisting within the same body in some Nestorian sense, but a unified substance – a divine-human nature. Only if the two natures were united in this way could the goodness of Christ's humanity be also seen as divine righteousness, God's redeeming gift to sinful humanity. In the same way, it enables the joyous exchange of our sin for his righteousness, in that it is as God that Jesus takes on our sin and overcomes it, and it is as man that he offers us a

---

[8]*LW* 44.38.
[9]Martin Luther, 'Disputation on the Divinity and Humanity of Christ', *D. Martin Luthers Werke: Kritische Gesamtausgabe,* 73 vols (Weimar: Böhlau, 1883), *WA* 39/2, pp. 92–121. Hereafter cited as *WA*.

perfect human righteousness, which is at the same time the right-eousness of God. It also preserved for Luther the notion that Jesus's human life and nature expressed perfectly the nature and heart of God. The incarnation, as God's gift of Christ to us, to be received by faith, is a true expression of the heart of God as turned towards humanity in love and favour. It reveals the innermost identity and will of God, not as the demanding judge, but as the generous giver. This is how we know what God is like. Furthermore, Luther always radically emphasized the true humanity of Christ, as a counter-point to late medieval tendencies towards Docetism. This tendency stemmed, for example, from the Christology of figures such as Hilary of Poitiers, who denied that Christ experienced pain in the Incarnation. This implicit failure to acknowledge the full human-ity of the incarnate Christ had led to a deficiency in his ability to relate to human experience, a gap quickly filled by devotion to the saints in popular spirituality. This all fed into a tendency to look to the example and prayers of the saints, taking attention away from Christ as the true object of faith, the one in whom alone our right-eousness is to be found.

Sacraments

This Christology and soteriology also affected Luther's understand-ing of the way God communicates himself to humankind: in a word, his sacramental theology. Luther originally clashed with Andreas Karlstadt over the interpretation of the mass or Lord's Supper, but later faced stronger opposition from Swiss theologians, particularly Huldrych Zwingli from Zürich, over the same issue. While Luther had long abandoned the medieval doctrine of transubstantiation as an unnecessary piece of speculative Aristotelian theory, he con-sistently held to the idea of the Real Presence, the notion that 'in the Supper we eat and take to ourselves Christ's body truly and physically'.[10] Zwingli, however, denied the real bodily presence of Christ in the elements of bread and wine, insisting that the Lord's Supper was primarily a communal meal, whereby Christians pledge their allegiance to both Christ and one another. A series of lengthy

---

[10]LW 37.28.

treatises and counter-treatises culminated in the Marburg Colloquy in which Philip of Hesse brought together the main figures in the evangelical movement at the time, including Luther, his close Wittenberg colleague Philip Melanchthon, Zwingli, Martin Bucer, Johannes Oecolampadius and Andreas Osiander. The debate was inconclusive. While agreement was acknowledged on a remarkably wide range of theological issues, over the contentious issue of sacramental presence, the parties agreed, reasonably amicably, to differ. Even so, it became clear in time that both still felt the fundamental issue had not been resolved. Zwingli thought Luther's insistence on the real bodily presence of Christ in the sacrament encouraged a false trust in the elements themselves rather than in Christ, and compromised God's spiritual freedom to act as he chooses, independent of physical forms. Luther thought Zwingli's refusal to recognize the embodied way in which God presents himself to us in sacraments was an implicit denial of the incarnation, and so jeopardized the reality of the gift of Christ to sinners.

At the heart of this sacramental argument lay Luther's ideas on merit, internal or external righteousness, and Christology. Justification consists of the promise and gift of the righteousness of Christ to sinners, received only by faith. Christologically, Luther could not conceive of any separation between Christ's divine and human nature, and so this gift of the external righteousness of Christ could not be thought of as just a spiritual entity, but had to take embodied form, just as in the incarnation. Hence, Luther thought of God's approach and availability to us in very physical forms. It is this Christological perspective that lies at the root of Luther's insistence on the real presence of Christ in the elements of bread and wine in the mass. God's word of promise, which comes in the form of both preaching and sacrament, not just refers to the gift of Christ, but also actually conveys what it promises. As he said about Andreas Karlstadt: 'He mocks us and brings us no further than to show us the holy thing in a glass or container. We can see it and smell it, until we are full, but ... he does not give it to us, he doesn't open it up, he doesn't allow it to be our own.' Justification is no mere legal fiction, but effects a real union between the believer and Christ at the most intimate level, in which the believer's sin is exchanged with Christ's righteousness. If, as Luther insists, Christ is one nature which is both human and divine then it cannot be that Christ is offered to us spiritually, while his physical presence or flesh is elsewhere.

Both belong together, and Christ and his benefits are offered to us bodily in the sacrament, to be received in faith. In the Lord's Supper, Christ is given to us, body and spirit, and this was crucial for Luther because justification consists precisely in the gift of Christ and his righteousness. If Christ is not present physically in the elements, he is not present at all. And if Christ is not given to us, there is no hope of salvation, because our merits can never achieve what is needed.

As we will see in Chapter 9, this view of justification also led him to a furious falling-out with the great Dutch humanist, Desiderius Erasmus. Erasmus advocated a simple freedom for the human will to choose to turn towards God or not, and stated his belief that further precision on such questions was impossible due to the lack of clarity of Scripture on these points. For Luther, this position was untenable on two main counts. First, it reopened the door to uncertainty in the doctrine of justification. If any part of justification was dependent on human action or choice, it reintroduced subjectivity and hence uncertainty, which robbed the sinner of the joyful certainty of God's grace and promise. Second, it undermined the clarity of Scripture. Only if the promise of Scripture was clear and unequivocal could it be trusted and hence bring security and peace. For Luther, Erasmus's casual assertion of Scripture's opaqueness on such questions removed the Christian's hope and freedom.

More pertinently, Erasmus's opinion undermined this sense that justification is based on the merits of Christ. The great humanist had argued that freedom of the will was vital, otherwise, no one would make an effort in the spiritual life and the commands of God were pointless. Luther responded by saying that this was precisely the point – we are not meant to make 'effort' for salvation; in fact, we must stop trying to produce good works that will merit grace and mercy, and instead learn to cast ourselves, without merits, on the merits of Christ.

The point could be laboured further through Luther's teaching on the Law and the Gospel, the two kingdoms' doctrine and many other tropes of Luther's theology. However, a purely historical answer is not enough. If we only give a historical answer to the question of the distinct nature of Luther's theology, then any commemoration of the Reformation can only ever be an antiquarian event, of interest to those involved in the historical development of theology or of European culture, but not of any abiding significance to the church or society today. In a world where few people are searching for a gracious God, are anxious about the threat of eternal punishment or want to know how to prepare for divine grace, what can Luther's theological revolution have to offer?

Justification and Self-Worth

It may be true that people today do not agonize over the questions Luther and his contemporaries did; however, questions of personal identity, worth and value remain as vital as ever. Many people in the modern world experience a constant demand to live up to standards of beauty set by the glamour industry, achievement set by business targets, or talent set by sporting or artistic success. Low self-esteem or negative self-worth is a persistent and difficult problem, occupying a great deal of time and energy on psychiatrists' couches. To have no sense of personal identity or to have a critically low sense of self-esteem is a crippling way to live. We need a sense of our own value and worth to be able to live confident, satisfying lives. The difficulty comes when we seek to find how such a sense of self-worth is established, because the truth is that our measures for such things are normally fully subjective and internal.[11]

Naturally, Luther was writing before the development of Freudian psychoanalysis or client-centred psychotherapy, yet his doctrine of justification by faith may have something to say to this very issue.

In the early sixteenth century, as we have seen, much popular spirituality, buttressed by theological emphases across the spectrum of late medieval thought, located the grounds of salvation in internal transformation, in the acquisition of merit or the *habitus* of virtue. Similarly, contemporary notions of salvation also demand internal change, the inheritance or acquisition of certain internal

---

[11]The historical roots of this may be found in what Charles Taylor called the 'subjective turn' in modern culture. Immanuel Kant's philosophy, e.g. was a 'turning inwards', finding moral imperative and grounds for action not in divine law or revelation, but in the resources of the ethical individual. We can only really be sure, not of divine revelation or of objective reality, but of our subjective appreciation of the world outside. Even Luther's theology was revised through Kantian eyes, leading to an equally subjective Luther, one whose key ideas were the power of faith or conscience. Luther himself, however, never really emphasized faith as a psychic power, or individual conscience as the focus of moral action. The focus for Luther, the object of faith, was not faith, or conscience, but Christ.

qualities that make a person feel or present themselves as worth-while. If you happen to be beautiful enough, thin enough, talented enough or intelligent enough, then you are thought to be worthy of attention, and can justifiably feel good about yourself. Even those not born with such qualities can remedy this with hard work: you may not look good, but if you are successful in business, in financial dealings or in sporting prowess, again that is the recipe for self-esteem and acceptability.

In other words, we too have our own version of 'internal right-eousness', the measure of success and self-worth. This is all very well, as long as looks, wealth or success lasts, but of course these things are in themselves inherently fragile. What happens when looks fade? When the business crashes? When sporting ability declines? Our news regularly reports on sporting stars who have found it difficult to cope with the end of their careers, descending into depression with their declining ability and the loss of atten-tion that success brought. The financial crash of 2008, like many before it, brought existential crisis to many whose sense of self was tied up with financial security and success. Spectacular falls from grace through public moral failure or scandal have led many into profound doubt and despair. What happens when the thing you are relying on to give you a sense of your own worth disappears?

Luther's doctrine of justification by the merits of another, sug-gests that true human worth lies not in any ability or quality we may or may not possess, but in the simple fact that we are loved by our Creator and declared acceptable in Christ. At the Heidelberg Disputation of 1518, Luther claimed that 'sinners are attractive because they are loved, they are not loved because they are attract-ive.'[12] In contemporary terms, Luther says that our true identity is not forged by ourselves, and our worth is not ultimately found in any particular quality we may happen to possess. It is not located in our looks, talent, wealth, reputation or anything internal to us at all: it is located in God's estimation of us as graced, loved and recipients of the gift of Christ. In short, our identity and self-worth are not self-generated or self-defined, but given. They are received as a gift, in the divine Word that declares us to be of value and worth, despite moral failure, physical flaws, and lack of talent and

[12]LW 31.57.

ability. In a world where identity is self-made and self-managed, where we rise or fall on the opinion of others, measured in retweets or Facebook likes, the news that our true selves are found in Christ, our true value is found in something external to ourselves, not internal, comes as good news, because it provides us with something sure, inviolable and reliable.

Luther often suggested that the mark of a good theology was whether it could hold you, not when times are good and life is going well, but when you are full of doubt, despair and trouble, when all around you is falling apart. Our contemporary gospel of achievement is bad theology, because a sense of worth built on personal qualities or achievements is always vulnerable to the changes and chances of shifting times and fortunes. Only a theology that offers something firm and steady, something that can hold you even when failure, age or disability strike, can provide a sure ground for peace and joy. Only a sense of value found in something external rather than internal can provide true shelter when the storm breaks.

Beyond this, Luther's doctrine of external righteousness reverses the way we tend to evaluate other people. If a person's value lies in an internal quality or feature that they possess, such as a particular skill or ability or racial characteristics, then it becomes possible to make distinctions between them on those grounds. Some people are more valuable and some are less. The disabled, the unproductive, the unemployed or the ugly are cast aside as worth little in the competitive race for attention. If, however, as Justification by Faith insists, a person's true value lies not in anything they possess but in something outside themselves – the fact that they are addressed and loved by God – then we cannot make such distinctions. Each person has dignity and value and deserves equal treatment regardless of age, skills, social utility or earning capacity.

The legacy of the Reformation is often sought in things such as individual freedom, universal education, the rise of human rights or the priority of individual conscience. In truth, while these may have been partially influenced by the Reformation, it is hard to argue they derive solely from this movement, or were particularly prominent in Luther's own thought. At the most they may be unintended consequences of the Reformation, under the influence of many other historical movements such as the Renaissance or the Enlightenment. Much more central is this idea of the location of human worth externally rather than internally. Luther still speaks today because he expresses an insight that goes to the heart of both modern and premodern insecurities and injustices: the joyful and liberating discovery that we do not need to establish our own or other people's worth or value from within ourselves, but it is given to us as a sheer gift.

2

Luther on Bible Translation

Luther's gospel, once discovered, began to change his entire view of the world. And this is particularly true of the work he was most pleased with, his translation of the Bible. Perhaps the two most influential documents that emerged from the Reformation period were Martin Luther's translation of the Bible into German, which finally appeared in full in 1534, and the English King James Version (KJV). Both had an extensive and profound effect on the languages into which they were translated. Luther combined the various forms of contemporary German into one common vernacular usage, which became the basis for a standardized spoken and written language for centuries to come. The KJV shaped the English language both in England itself and, in time, throughout the world in the various British colonies, as British traders and missionaries took the King James Bible with them on their overseas ventures in subsequent centuries. And, as we shall see, Luther's gospel profoundly influenced his approach to translating the Bible, and helps us recognize the differences between his work and that of the translators of the KJV.

There is, of course, a vital link between the two: William Tyndale. Tyndale learnt German specifically to read and to use Luther's translation. If one account of Tyndale's life is to be believed, after his appeal to Bishop Tunstall for patronage of the idea for a new translation had been turned down, he visited Wittenberg in 1525 to familiarize himself with what was happening there, and presumably to meet Luther himself, before relocating to the low countries. Despite the fact that he took a different approach to translation from Luther, Tyndale's subsequent translation was significantly influenced by Luther's. In some estimates, 76 percent of the Old

Testament and 84 percent of the New Testament language in the KJV derives from Tyndale, duly passed through the filter of the various versions of Coverdale, Geneva, the Bishops' Bible and so on. Therefore, some of Luther's translation found its way indirectly into the King James Bible from Tyndale. Heinz Bluhm's work in the 1960s indicated a number of instances of how phraseology and language in Luther's translation, turned into parallel English prose, found its way via Coverdale to the King James Bible.[1] This is not to say, however, that the translations are the same, or take the same approach. As we will see, despite the fact that they both emerge out of the European Reformation, they take a very distinct and different approach to the task of translation, rooted in turn in very different theological and contextual starting points.

Martin Luther's Approach to Bible Translation

After his appearance before the emperor at the Diet of Worms in 1521, Luther was spirited away for his own safety to the Wartburg Castle, not far from one of his childhood homes in Eisenach. There, he began the task of translating the Bible into German, with the New Testament appearing in 1522 (working from Erasmus's new edition of the Greek New Testament), and the full Bible finally in 1534.

Luther wrote about the task of, and his approach to, Bible translation in two main documents. One was his *Sendbrief von Dolmetschen*, or 'An Open Letter on Translating', written while he waited at Coburg Castle for the outcome of the Diet of Augsburg in 1530. In September that year, his New Testament had come in for severe criticism, especially for his translation of Romans 3:28, when he inserted a word not found in the Greek – the word '*allein*'. So, a verse that in the NRSV reads: 'For we hold that a person is justified by faith apart from works prescribed by the law' was rendered in Luther's version: '*So halten wir es nu, das der Mensch gerecht werde, on des Gesetzes werck,* alleine *durch den Glauben*' ('without

---

[1]Heinz Bluhm, *Martin Luther: Creative Translator* (St Louis: Concordia, 1965), ch. 9.

works of the law, through faith *alone*'). The '*Sendbrief*' was in part a defence of this decision and in part an explanation of his broader convictions about the task of Bible translation.

The other key document is his 'Defence of the Translation of the Psalms', written in 1531, and finally published in December 1532. He also touched on the task in several instances of 'Table Talk', which give valuable brief insights into his approach to translation. From these documents, three central themes appear, referring to the requirements of a good translation, and a good translator, of the Bible.

An Idiomatic Translation

Luther's Bible was very significant for the German language, but it was by no means the first German translation. The first vernacular Bible in Europe had been produced in Strasbourg in 1466 in German. By 1507, thirteen further German editions had been produced as well as five different versions of the Psalms. Between 1477 and 1522, four Lower German editions of the Bible had also appeared. Luther therefore did not decide to translate because no German translation existed. Like the translators of the KJV, he wanted to improve on what was available. However, unlike them, he started directly from the Hebrew and Greek texts rather than using previous editions of the Bible as a starting point. Most significant was his desire to make a truly localized, colloquial German translation. His criticisms of these previous German versions centred on their inaccessibility to ordinary people. As he put it in his 'Prefaces to the Old Testament':

> Nor have I read, up to this time, a book or letter which contained the right kind of German. Besides no one pays any attention to speaking real German. This is especially true of the people in the chancelleries, as well as those patchwork preachers and wretched writers.[2]

For Luther, the primary requirement for a translator of the Bible was not, strangely enough, expert knowledge of Greek and Hebrew,

---

[2]*LW* 35.250.

but an excellent knowledge of idiomatic German. For him, close familiarity with the receptor language was as important, if not more important, than knowledge of the donor languages. The aim was to find the most idiomatic way of expressing the sense of the biblical text, in a way that people who speak that colloquial language can understand and follow. In this way, Luther established what John Flood called 'the emancipation of the vernacular' from the hold that the classical languages had on German culture up until that point.[3] In the 'Sendbrief', he writes:

> I wanted to speak German, not Latin or Greek, since it was German I had undertaken to speak in the translation ... We do not have to inquire of the literal Latin, how we are to speak German as these asses do. Rather we must inquire about this of the mother in the home, the children on the street, the common man in the marketplace. We must be guided by their language, the way they speak, and do our translating accordingly.[4]

The translator learns to translate not by reading Hebrew but by listening to people: 'Therefore I must let the literal word go, and try to learn how the German says that which the Hebrew expresses.'[5] In his 'Defence of the Translation of the Psalms', he writes: 'Once he has the German words to serve purpose, let him drop the Hebrew words and express himself freely in the best German he knows.'[6] His defence of the insertion of the word '*alleine*' in Romans 3:28 is at least in part a linguistic argument, claiming that colloquial German requires the '*allein – kein*' construction in comparing and contrasting two things.[7]

Luther often argues against the value of a direct word-for-word translation. For example, in his Preface to the book of Job, written in 1545, he states:

---

[3]John L. Flood, 'Martin Luther's Bible Translation in Its German and European Context', *The Bible in the Renaissance: Essays on Biblical Commentary and Translation in the Fifteenth and Sixteenth Centuries* (Aldershot: Ashgate, 2001), p. 48.
[4]*LW* 35.189.
[5]*LW* 35.193.
[6]*LW* 35.214.
[7]*LW* 35.188.

The language of this book is more vigorous and splendid than that of any other book in all the Scriptures. Yet if it were translated everywhere word for word – as the Jews and foolish translators would have it done – and not for the most part according to the sense, no one would understand it.[8]

Literal, word-for-word translations often obscure rather than reveal. And because Scripture is meant to reveal God, understanding is vital, so the translator must feel free to stay closer to a comprehensible form in the receptor language rather than leave obscurities unresolved in the donor language.

Luther therefore takes very seriously the context in which a translation takes place. For him, this includes both the linguistic context and the historical one. The second reason he gives for his inclusion of '*allein*' in Romans 3:28 is the need for theological clarification in the polemical circumstances of the sixteenth century. This addition is needed, he says, 'especially in these days, for they have been accustomed to works so long they have to be torn away from them by force. For these reasons it is not only right but also highly necessary to speak it out as plainly and fully as possible'.[9]

Behind all this, there lies a significant principle: that in translation the vital thing is not a direct rendering of the original language, but the conveying of the idea behind the original language in ordinary speech. This, of course, assumes that it is possible to identify the ideas behind the words, which leads to Luther's second key principle in Bible translation.

A Theological Translation

For Luther, a translation needs to express the heart of the message of Scripture, which for him, as we have seen, is the message of an external righteousness, the justifying righteousness of Christ, received by faith alone. He describes the task of translation like the hard work of clearing a field of stones and boulders: 'We had to sweat and toil there before we got those boulders and clods out of the way, so that one could go along so nicely. The plowing goes well

---

[8]*LW* 35.252.
[9]*LW* 35.198.

when the field is cleared. But rooting out the woods and stumps, and getting the field ready – this is a job nobody wants.'[10] The image conveys the idea of finding a rough field, full of obstacles that need to be cleared away. Similarly, the Bible presents a number of linguistic and theological problems that need to be ironed out, cleared up, made smooth. And in order to do this work, the translator needs to be a good theologian, one who understands the gospel.

While Luther wants good idiomatic German, even that is subservient to the overall theological goal: 'I preferred to do violence to the German language rather than to depart from the word.'[11] If his first two reasons for the insertion of '*allein*' into Romans 3:28 were linguistic and historical, the third was theological:

> For in that very passage he is dealing with the main point of Christian doctrine, namely, that we are justified by faith in Christ without any works of the law. And Paul cuts away all works so completely, as even to say that the works of the law – though it is God's law and word – do not help us for justification ... But when all works are so completely cut away – and that must mean that faith alone justifies – whoever would speak plainly and clearly about this cutting away of works will have to say, 'Faith alone justifies us, and not works.' The matter itself, as well as the nature of the language, demands it.[12]

A text that displays the dynamic at work here is James 2:24 – 'You see that a person is justified by what he does and not by faith alone' (New International Version) – a verse that could be fatal to Luther's interpretation of the gospel. At first glance, he translates it fairly 'straight': '*So sehet ihr nun, daß der Mensch durch die Werke gerecht wird, nicht durch den Glauben allein.*' The key phrase 'not through faith alone' is translated directly. However, there is a twist in the tail. In his translation of the verb 'justify', he makes a subtle shift from a clearly present tense (in the Greek) to a tense that, if not exactly future, still implies an ongoing process that is not yet finished (in the German – *gerecht wird*). The 'justification' referred to thus becomes eschatological. Luther's understanding of justification

---

[10]Ibid.
[11]*LW* 35.194.
[12]*LW* 35.195.

was that God's righteousness is given to us in Christ now, as an anticipation of the final declaration of righteousness to be pronounced one day on us.[13] The subtle shift of the tense to indicate an ongoing process allows him to shift the focus of the verse. It moves from the declaration of justification in the present (in which no works are involved) to the final state of being justified in the future, the final delivery from all sin, which will involve a certain level of discipline and, in one sense, 'works'. It is a small shift, but a significant one, guided by his prior theological understanding.

When there are disputed readings, the crucial guiding hand in Luther's translation is his understanding of the heart of the gospel. Where the meaning of the text is unclear, Luther usually seeks to translate it in ways that fit his theological framework. There are a number of examples of this.

First, in Romans 1:17, another seminal verse for Luther, as it had sparked his own 'Reformation breakthrough', the Greek simply has the phrase δικαιοσύνη θεοῦ. This could, of course, mean 'the righteousness which God possesses', 'the righteousness God requires' or even 'the justice of God'. Luther translates it with the phrase '*die Gerechtigkeit, die vor Gott gilt*' (the righteousness that counts before God), making it very clear in what sense he wants the phrase to be read, one that ties in with his notion of 'external righteousness', given to us by God.

Second, there is the famous Lutheran distinction between 'law' and 'gospel' that dictates the resulting translation. One saying recorded in the 'Table Talk' reports:

If some passage is obscure I consider whether it treats of grace or of law, whether wrath or the forgiveness of sin [is contained in it], and with which of these it agrees better. By this procedure I have often understood the most obscure passages. Either the law or the gospel has made them meaningful, for God divides his teaching into law and gospel.[14]

---

[13]e.g. in Luther's Romans commentary he writes of the believer that 'he is at the same time both a sinner and a righteous man; a sinner in fact, but a righteous man by the sure imputation and promise of God that He will continue to deliver him from sin until He has completely cured him. And thus he is entirely healthy in hope.' *LW* 25.260.

[14]LW 54.42.

Third, in a different fragment from the Table Talk, yet another of Luther's devices for interpretation, the three 'orders', is decisive:

> The Bible speaks and teaches about the works of God. About this there is no doubt. These works are divided in three hierarchies: the household, the government, the church. If a verse does not fit the church, we should let it stay in the government or the household, whichever it is best suited to.[15]

Fourth, Luther is convinced that the heart of the Bible's message is Christ. In his Preface to the Old Testament of 1545, he writes:

> The Hebrew language, sad to say, has gone down so far that even the Jews know little enough about it, and their glosses and interpretations (which I have tested) are not to be relied upon. I think that if the Bible is to come up again, we Christians are the ones who must do the work, for we have the understanding of Christ without which even the knowledge of the language is nothing. Because they were without it, the translators of old, even Jerome, made mistakes in many passages. Though I cannot boast of having achieved perfection, nevertheless, I venture to say that this German Bible is clearer and more accurate at many points than the Latin. So it is true that if the printers do not, as usual, spoil it with their carelessness, the German language certainly has here a better Bible than the Latin language – and the readers will bear me out in this.[16]

This bold claim that his German Bible is clearer than Jerome's is not a claim to be a better translator but a better theologian. Luther believes that his rediscovery of the centrality of Christ and his right-eousness, received by faith, as the heart of the message of Scripture makes his Bible clearer in the sense that the light of the gospel shines out more clearly from it than it does from Jerome's Latin translation.[17]

---

[15]LW 54.446.

[16]LW 35.249.

[17]Friedrich Kantzenbach makes the point that it was the centrality of Christ to Scripture that shapes Luther's translation throughout: 'Luther's Bible Translation is consequently the fruit of his struggle over the truth of the Gospel. It took a long journey until Luther could find *one* theme which Holy Scripture showed forth in

Luther therefore strives for a Christological translation that conveys this central idea. When translating difficult Old Testament texts, he says: 'Whenever equivocal words or constructions occur, that one would have to be taken which (without, however, doing injustice to the grammar) agrees with the New Testament.'[18] Luther rejects Jewish exegesis of the Old Testament, because it fails to recognize Christ as the centre of Scripture:

> For we followed the rule that wherever the words could have given or tolerated an improved meaning, there we did not allow ourselves to be forced by the artificial Hebrew of the rabbis into accepting a different inferior meaning ... words are to serve and follow the meaning, and not meaning the words.[19]

That final sentence goes to the heart of Luther's approach to Bible translation. For Luther, a good translation always elucidates the heart of the gospel. Again, the focus is not on the individual words of Scripture, but on a translation that conveys the heart of the message of the Bible.

A Faith-ful Translator

Besides a knowledge of colloquial German and a grasp of the essentials of the gospel, Luther has one other chief quality that he expects of a translator: 'Translating is not every man's skill as the mad saints imagine. It requires a right, devout, honest, sincere, God-fearing, Christian, trained, informed, and experienced heart. Therefore I hold that no false Christian or factious spirit can be a decent translator.'[20] Translation does not just require a good theological knowledge, but also needs a certain experience of grace.

Luther's theology of the cross, developed in his early years, yet continuing to influence his theology throughout his career,

---

all its variety, its different literary types and methods of teaching, namely Christ.' Friedrich Kantzenbach, 'Luthers Sprache Der Bible', in Hans Volz (ed.), *Martin Luthers Deutsch Bibel* (Hamburg: Friedrich Wittig Verlag, 1978), p. 13.
[18] *LW* 54.446.
[19] *LW* 35.213.
[20] *LW* 35.194.

emphasizes the place of experience in theology. As he puts it in his *Operationes super Psalterium* of 1519–21: 'Let no-one think himself a theologian if he has read, understood and taught these things … It is living, or rather dying and being damned that makes a theologian, not understanding, reading and speculating.'[21]

For Luther, the experience of being radically humbled, brought to the end of one's own resources, leads to faith, in that it teaches the futility of relying on one's own works, achievements and abilities, and instead leads a person to cry out to God for mercy, lifting up hands not full of works, but the empty hands of faith. This is why true theology begins at the cross for Luther, and by 'cross' he often means the experience of suffering: 'Therefore we should know that God hides Himself under the form of the worst devil. This teaches us that the goodness, mercy, and power of God cannot be grasped by speculation but must be understood on the basis of experience.'[22]

Experience, notably the experience of despair, temptation and doubt teach the Christian not to rely on his or her own resources, but to simply trust the promise of God that he saves and rescues sinners. In this way, experience is the true teacher of theology. No one can understand true Christian theology unless they have undergone this radical humbling, this personal experience of what he would often call '*Anfechtung*', leading to abandonment of self-reliance and instead faith in Christ alone. Translation requires good theology and good theology requires not just academic expertise or learning, but also personal faith. This is why, as mentioned above, translation 'requires a right, devout, honest, sincere, God-fearing, Christian, trained, informed, and experienced heart'.[23] Experience is vital for the making of a good theologian and therefore a good translator, partly at least because a good translation, which properly understands the distinction between law and gospel, aims to reproduce that same experience in the hearts of its readers. The goal of a translation of Scripture is not just understanding, but also faith.

---

[21]'*Vivendo, immo moriendo et damnando fit theologus, non intelligendo, legendo aut speculando*', WA 2.296.8–11.
[22]*LW* 7.175.
[23]*LW* 35.194.

Conclusion: Luther and the Task of Translation

Translation requires a good knowledge of the idiomatic receptor language, a theologically astute mind that has understood the essence of the gospel and experience of grace. These are the distinguishing marks of Luther's approach to Bible translation.

In all these cases, attention is drawn away from the very words of Scripture, the *ipsissima verba*, to the meaning behind it, to the theological and Christological heart of Scripture, and to the experience of humbling that leads to faith. The emphasis for Luther lies not in the original words themselves, but in the gospel they express: 'Words are to serve and follow the meaning, and not meaning the words.'[24] In his mind the two main poles of the work of Bible translation are the internal message of the Scriptures and the person who hears them, understood in all the particularities of their social and linguistic context. The actual words of Scripture seem to recede into the background, in the shadow of his desire to communicate an idea to an audience.

The Approach to Bible Translation in the King James Version

In stark contrast to Luther's defiant and independent tone, the Preface to the KJV feels very different. Its deferential opening, flattering King James, the 'most dread Sovereign' with mention of the blessings God has poured out on the nation through him, indicates that, if it is an exaggeration to say that the KJV was written for an audience of one, that particular reader loomed large in the thoughts of the translators. Here, we will again seek to draw out some key themes of the translation approach in this text.

There are many similarities in the two translations. Like Luther, the KJV disdains the use of too many marginal comments. The translators allow themselves to indulge only where there are variant readings touching on non-essential doctrines. By contrast, the Geneva Bible was marked by its many theological stage directions,

---

[24]*LW* 35.213.

indicating how the text was to be read in a duly Calvinist manner. In the Preface to the Geneva Bible, the translators indicate that their approach was to have 'faithfully rendered the text and in all hard places most sincerely expounded the same ... as we have chiefly observed the sense, and laboured to keep the propriety of the words'.[25] At the same time, they took care to add what they euphemistically called 'brief annotations' to help the reader understand. The Geneva Bible, like Luther, has a particular theological framework, a set of convictions as to the core message of Scripture. Contrary to Luther, it relies heavily on the marginal notes rather than the translation itself to convey the convictions of the translators, who felt duty bound to translate the text in a fairly literal or exact way. Luther, on the other hand, relies more on the translation itself to carry the theological weight of conveying the true message of Scripture without extensive marginal notes. He feels more free to depart from a literal translation for the purposes of idiomatic German expression of the message and to convey the meaning behind the actual words.

The KJV translators take a still different approach. Richard Bancroft's terse sixth Rule for the Translators had made the policy plain: 'No marginal notes at all to be affixed, but only for the explanation of the Hebrew or Greek words, which cannot without some circumlocution so briefly and fitly be expressed in the text.' The emphasis here is on 'at all'. There are to be neither Calvinist marginal notes nor, for that matter, notes advocating royal supremacy. The translation is to observe a strict neutrality. However, they omit marginal notes for reasons different from Luther. It is not because they hope to convey a distinct theological context within the text of the translation, but because suggesting a distinct theological standpoint is not a primary consideration for them.

The 'Epistle Dedicatory' to the Preface to the KJV positions the translation deliberately between the poles of early seventeenth-century English religion:

> If on the one side, we shall be traduced by Popish Persons at home or abroad, who therefore will malign us, because we are poor instruments to make God's holy Truth to be yet more and

---

[25]Preface to the Geneva Bible, 1560, in Gerald Bray (ed.), *Documents of the English Reformation* (Cambridge: James Clarke, 1994), p. 361.

more known unto the people, whom they desire still to keep
in ignorance and darkness; or if, on the other side, we shall be
maligned by self-conceited Brethren, who run their own ways,
and give liking unto nothing, but what is framed by themselves,
and hammered on their anvil; we may rest secure, supported
within by truth and innocence of a good conscience, having
walked the ways of simplicity and integrity, as before the Lord;
and sustained without by the powerful protection of Your
Majesty's grace and favour, which will ever give countenance
to honest and Christian endeavours against bitter censures and
uncharitable imputations.[26]

The path set out is not theological, but moral and spiritual: 'the
ways of simplicity and integrity', duly guarded by royal protection.
The aim is not a theological translation in the sense that Luther's
is, but rather one that aims at 'simplicity and integrity'. In other
words, the aim is a simple and understandable translation (simplicity), which is as accurate and faithful a translation as possible
of the original texts (integrity). The point is developed in Smith's
Preface where he explains the decision not to render each Hebrew
or Greek word with exactly the same English word in each instance:

We have not tied ourselves to an uniformity of phrasing, or to an
identity of words, as some peradventure would wish that we had
done ... Thus to mince the matter, we thought to savour more
of curiosity than wisdom, and that rather it would breed scorn
in the Atheist, than bring profit to the godly Reader. For is the
kingdom of God to become words or syllables? Why should we
be in bondage to them if we may be free, use one precisely when
we may use another no less fit, as commodiously?[27]

Here is a striving for an exact phrasing that does justice to the
original, but that avoids a stilted awkwardness that would come
from sticking to the exact correspondence of each Hebrew or Greek
word with the same English one on every occasion. The concern
here is for two things: a 'commodious' translation and a precise
one. There is a delicate striving for a careful balance. On one hand,

---

[26]Ibid., pp. 415–16.
[27]Ibid., pp. 434–5.

if a word means the same, they feel they should translate it with the same word. However, they do not feel themselves tied to that as a rigid rule, because it then becomes 'mincing the matter' – something 'curious', odd and obscure.

Absent from both Bancroft's Rules and Smith's Preface is any sense of a distinct theological vision driving the translators. Naturally, Smith's slightly fawning address to King James shows that little quarter will be given to Calvinist subversion of royal rule, and Bancroft's third Rule for the Translators – 'Old ecclesiastical words to be kept, namely, as the word *church* not to be translated *congregation* etc.' – directed them to avoid Tyndale's separatist leanings. Apart from that, however, neither shows any interest in a driving prior understanding of the gospel, as lies behind both Luther's version and the Geneva Bible.

Also absent is any sense of a desire to express the Bible in colloquial English. Contrary to Luther, the selection of members of the companies of translators of the KJV focused on their ability to handle the donor languages, rather than the receptor one. As Smith put it: 'Therefore such were thought upon, as could say modestly with Saint Jerome, "Both we have learned the Hebrew tongue in part, and in the Latin we have been exercised almost from our very cradle."'[28] Jerome himself is praised as 'the best linguist, without controversy, of his age, or of any that went before him'.[29] It is these more technical qualities, rather than familiarity with idiomatic English, or even personal experience of grace that primarily qualifies a person to be a translator. In addition, the requirement to work from the Bishops' Bible, except where it was misleading, led to the KJV retaining archaic forms of English that were, in fact, already going out of use in the early seventeenth century, such as the personal forms of address: *thou*, *thee* and *thy*, instead of *you*, *your* and *yours*.[30] Luther would never have countenanced such an approach.

David Norton's analysis of the KJV concluded that 'textual accuracy, theological neutrality and political acceptability were the qualities desired, and the aim a single generally acceptable

---

[28]Ibid., p. 432.

[29]Ibid., p. 422.

[30]Alister McGrath, *In the Beginning: The Story of the King James Bible and How It Changed a Nation, a Language and a Culture* (New York: Doubleday, 2001), pp. 266–71.

text'.[31] And again, 'the translators were not concerned with qualities in their English other than fidelity to the original'.[32] The KJV
shows no great interest in either a colloquial translation or a
theological one. A couple of examples will bear this out: Luther himself cites the
angelic greeting to Mary in Luke 1:28 as a case in point where the
Latin misses the mark. It may be worth laying out each version in
turn to make the point:

GREEK: καὶ εἰσελθὼν πρὸς αὐτὴν εἶπεν, Χαῖρε, κεχαριτωμένη, ὁ
κύριος μετὰ σοῦ.

VULGATE: et ingressus angelus ad eam dixit: ave gratia plena,
Dominus tecum benedicta tu in mulieribus

LUTHER: Und der Engel kam zu jr hin ein und sprach: Gegrüsset
seistu holdselige, der Herr ist mit dir du Gebenedeitete unter
den Weibern.

KJV: And the angel came in unto her, and said, Hail, *thou that
art* highly favoured, the Lord is with thee: blessed art thou
among women.

Luther complains that the clumsy Latin '*gratia plena*' would make a
German 'think of a keg "full of" beer or a purse "full of" money'.[33]
His theology of grace wanted to avoid any sense that grace was a
substance that could be dished out by the papacy in the form of
indulgences or merits. Instead grace is simply God's favour towards
us. So he feels free to depart from the Greek significantly, with his
more colloquial '*Gegrüsset seistu holdselige*' (literally, 'you are
greeted, gracious one').

The KJV also departs from the Greek (and the Latin, for that
matter), but for different reasons. It has the phrase 'hail, *thou that
art* highly favoured'. It uses six words to convey what the Greek
does in two, the Latin in three and Luther also in three. The KJV is
striving for as faithful a rendering as possible, even indicating to the
reader that the words 'thou that art' are not strictly speaking there

---

[31]David Norton, *A History of the Bible as Literature* (Cambridge: Cambridge
University Press, 1993), pp. 144–5.
[32]Ibid., p. 157.
[33]*LW* 35.191.

in the Greek by the use of Roman type, rather than black letter type (in later versions in italics) so that the reader can keep as close to the original as possible. They are content to expand the text, while avoiding the unfortunate spatial and substantial connotations of the Latin, and the chatty colloquialism of Luther. The resulting phrase 'hail, thou that art highly favoured' sounds less idiomatic, yet still has a smooth rhythm, with syllabic variety and a certain literary beauty to it. The departure from an exact rendering of the Greek is not for the sake of idiomatic English, but for a certain precise dignity. It is a phrase that captures what Adam Nicolson calls the 'passionate exactness' of the KJV.[34]

A different, but equally illuminating, example is Psalm 58:9. In the KJV we find 'before your pots can feel the thorns, he shall take them away as in a whirlwind, both living and in his wrath'. It is a sentence that has balance and rhythm, is a fairly literal translation, yet it makes little sense. We can sense the perplexity of the translators, as the Hebrew at this point is difficult to translate, as most modern versions acknowledge in marginal notes. Luther instead has *'Ehe ewre Dornen reiff werden am Dornstrauche, wird sie dein zorn so Frisch wegreisen'*, or roughly translated: 'Before your thorns have ripened on the thornbush, your wrath will tear them out while they are still green.' Here, Luther feels free to depart from the Hebrew to give a comprehensible sentence, while the KJV translators would prefer to offer something barely meaningful, yet closer to the original. Luther's version is idiomatic and conveys a clear idea of divine judgement – a depiction of the law, not the gospel. The KJV line is rhythmically balanced and flows delicately, yet has no theological idea driving it, and is happier to offer the reader what is on the page of the Hebrew, rather than forcing it into a colloquial phrase.

Conclusion: The Bible – Familiar or Strange?

What then can we conclude about the difference of approaches in these two translations, arguably the two most influential texts that emerged from the era of the Reformation?

---

[34]Norton, *A History of the Bible as Literature*, p. 197.

Paul Ricoeur's essay 'On Translation' argues that the perfect translation is a false ideal, born out of an Enlightenment confidence in the exact reference of language to meaning. The supposed dilemma between faithfulness to and betrayal of a text is false: every translation is in some sense a betrayal. We are to 'give up the ideal of the perfect translation'. In one sense, translation is impossible but we still do it.[35]

Luther probably would have agreed. For him, no translation is neutral. His version of the Bible is an unashamedly Lutheran one, conveying a particular understanding of the gospel, with justification by faith, law and gospel, the two kingdoms, all the classic Lutheran ideas running throughout. He also wants to make the biblical writers sound like Germans, to embed the text in the culture and the language of his people and his time. It is a translation that makes the biblical text close, intimate, contemporary, blended with the language of the market and the home. In 1528, Luther wrote to Wenceslas Linck:

> We are sweating over the work of putting the Prophets into German. God, how much of it there is, and how hard it is to make these Hebrew writers talk German! They resist us, and do not want to leave their Hebrew and imitate our German barbarisms. It is like making a nightingale leave her own sweet song and imitate the monotonous voice of a cuckoo, which she detests.[36]

Just like contemporary artists who painted biblical scenes with characters in sixteenth-century clothes, Luther wants to overcome the sense of distance and unfamiliarity of the text, to help people find themselves and their language in the stories of the Bible, to make God speak German. It is a translation of immanence rather than of transcendence, of incarnation into German culture that fits the Christological core of his gospel.

The KJV translators, on the other hand, preserve more of the strangeness of the scriptural text. Here, there is no attempt to make Amos sound like a Hampshire farmer or Luke a London physician.

---

[35]Paul Ricoeur, *On Translation, Thinking in Action* (London: Routledge, 2006), p. 12.
[36]*LW* 35.229.

It makes the Bible (and perhaps God) seem less immediate, more alien, aloof, yet also more majestic, 'awesome', in the older sense of that word. Adam Nicolson's book on the KJV argues that this English Bible refuses to make a choice between the Cavalier richness of ceremony and the Puritan austerity of simplicity. What he does not include is the intimacy of nearness, the sense that the Bible speaks our language, relates directly to our concerns – something that Luther's translation does more effectively.

The KJV trusts the reader more, offering him or her the information they need – as exact a translation as is possible while retaining a sense of style and 'commodiousness'. Unlike papally approved versions, the KJV translators were content to insert marginal notes indicating variant readings of a text, leaving uncertainties as uncertainties and giving the reader the opportunity to make up their own mind. It avoids controversy, refusing to side with a particular interpretation of the Bible, instead giving the reader room for manoeuvre, a classically Anglican thing to do.

The differences are of emphasis rather than total contrast. However, the two versions embody a number of different strands of the Reformation movement. If the Reformation was in part a democratization of religion, making it accessible and familiar, giving people a gracious God that they could love rather than fear, then Luther's translation conveyed all that and more. At the same time, however, the Reformation also bequeathed a strong sense of freedom of conscience, of the exaltation of the laity, giving them every right to read the Scripture and make up their mind about it as the priests and the scholars. And it is this aspect that is best preserved in the KJV.

The translations also are products of their age. Luther's breathes the atmosphere of the early years of the Reformation, with his initial confidence that the gospel had now been discovered and now needed only to be proclaimed far and wide for it to be welcomed and believed. The KJV breathes the more nervous and cautious air of a century later, a century of sobering division and dispute that made it clear that biblical interpretation and finding unanimity was not as straightforward as it had seemed in those heady days of the 1520s.

Around forty years after the KJV was published, William Chillingworth wrote his famous line: 'The Bible, I say, the Bible only, is the religion of Protestants.'[37] It sounds like the kind of thing Luther would have said. Chillingworth, however, probably meant it in a different way – that the Bible, rather than any particular interpretation of the Bible, is what Protestants cling to. That, Luther would not have agreed with. Therein lies the dilemma of the Reformation, and these two versions together capture both the richness and the vigour, yet also the tensions that lie at the heart of this movement that has shaped the modern world so extensively.

---

[37]William Chillingworth, *The Religion of Protestants* (London: Bell & Daldy, 1870), p. 463.

3

Luther on Paul

Reminiscing on the early part of his career in his Preface to the Latin translation of his works, Martin Luther famously attributed the origins of his Reformation discovery to his new reading of Romans 1:17. As far as he saw it, the Reformation had been a return to preeminence of the theology of 'The Bible and St Augustine' rather than the intricacies of medieval scholastics of various kinds, such as Aquinas, Lombard or Biel. His reading of the Bible was shaped by the series of lectures he gave in his role as professor of Holy Scripture in the University of Wittenberg during these early years, and lectures on the Psalms, Romans, Galatians and Hebrews. The list leans heavily on St Paul, and bearing in mind the significance of his struggles with this text in Romans, we may fairly imagine that by his reference to 'the Bible' he largely meant St Paul. Until comparatively recently, at least in Protestant circles, Luther has been seen as the closest bedfellow of St Paul, the supreme interpreter of the apostle as the teacher of Justification by Faith. Before Luther, no one in theological history had accorded such a focus on the single doctrine of Justification as the central chapter of doctrine. It seemed to many as if Paul had been born again along with Luther. No longer, however.

The 'New Perspective on Paul' (NP for short from here on), although of course no longer so new, has long been seen as driving a wedge between Paul and Luther.[1] As early as 1961, Krister Stendahl lectured on the 'Introspective Conscience of the West' and distanced Paul from the kind of agonizing self-consciousness he saw

---

[1] I am grateful to my colleague Dr Chris Tilling for his advice on some of the scholarly issues connected with the NP in this chapter. Needless to say, any errors remaining are mine, not his.

in Luther. For him, within Protestantism, 'the Pauline awareness of sin has been interpreted in the light of Luther's struggle with his conscience.'[2] Stendahl's view was that until Augustine, Paul was thought to be writing about issues such as the law, the Temple, and the relationship between Jews and Gentiles now that Christ has come. It was with Augustine that he began to be read in terms of psychological introversion, and 'the Augustinian line leads into the Middle Ages and reaches its climax in the penitential struggle of an Augustinian monk, Martin Luther and in his interpretation of St Paul.'[3] Thus, Stendahl saw a 'radical difference' between Luther and Paul, due to this loss of the true Pauline concern with the relations between Jew and Gentile in the new age inaugurated by the coming of the messiah, and a turn towards the resolution of the inner turmoil of an anguished Augustine or Luther.

Ever since then, as the NP has developed, Paul has increasingly been pitted against Luther. A new understanding of Paul has emerged that distances him strongly from the great Reformer.[4] These days you have to be either for Paul or for Luther. You either side with the NP and say Luther got Paul wrong, or side with Luther and say the NP got Paul wrong. If you are drawn to the NP as making greater sense of Paul, then it seems you have to say farewell to Luther.

However, might this opposition itself be mistaken? Can some of the main NP themes be harmonized with Luther's teaching? This chapter suggests that not only there is such a way, but also Luther's teaching has a lot more in common with the NP than is usually thought. Perhaps the 'Old Perspective' got both Paul and Luther wrong? Or more likely, the understanding of Luther in the NP is somewhat lacking (not surprising, given that most of its proponents are New Testament, not Reformation, scholars) and this has led to a too rapid rejection of Luther among the followers of the NP. Moreover, many of the self-styled defenders of Luther have also missed important aspects of his teaching that are, in fact, not far from the concerns of the NP. If the 'Old Perspective' placed Paul firmly alongside Luther, and the NP has split them apart, perhaps

---

[2]Krister Stendahl, *Paul among Jews and Gentiles* (Philadelphia: Fortress Press, 1976), p. 79.
[3]Ibid., p. 85.
[4]E.g. in E. P. Sanders, *Paul* (New York: Oxford University Press, 1991) and cf. also Stephen Westerholm, *Perspectives Old and New on Paul: The 'Lutheran' Paul and His Critics* (Grand Rapids: Eerdmans, 2004).

it is time for them to be reunited in a new angle on the NP. Perhaps Luther did understand Paul after all.

Now, of course, the further we look into the NP, the more varied and broad it becomes. Apart from the general rejection of charges of legalism (building on Sanders's 'covenantal nomism'), it is increasingly difficult to harmonize the views of different scholars who would be seen as proponents of the NP into a coherent set of ideas. This chapter therefore picks on one NP scholar, N. T. Wright, partly because he is perhaps one of the best-known figures in the United Kingdom in this area, at least at a more popular level, and because his reading of Paul has recently been criticized precisely for having departed from a Reformation understanding of the apostle. Critiques of the NP come either as a robust defence of the older, supposedly Reformation emphases, trying to show that Paul was a Lutheran (or perhaps Calvinist) after all,[5] or trying to show some of the misunderstandings of Luther current in some of the writers of the NP.[6] This issue has recently come into focus in the debate between John Piper and N. T. Wright, which has become a major trans-Atlantic argument, occupying the minds of all kinds of blogs and message boards.[7] However, here I hope to show that Luther's gospel, in fact, shows an understanding of Paul that is not that far away from that seen in N. T. Wright's reading of Paul (and in aspects of James Dunn), given the different historical contexts in which these theologies emerged. Luther's reading of Paul shows his gospel at work.

N. T. Wright on Paul

Among the key tenets of Wright's understanding of Paul are the following:

1. *An eschatological understanding of justification:* δικαιοσύνη, as Paul uses it, is understood not as a quality of life God demands from humans in order to justify them, but is

---

[5] e.g. John Piper, *The Future of Justification: A Response to N. T. Wright* (Wheaton: Crossway, 2006).

[6] E.g. Wilfried Härle, 'Rethinking Paul and Luther', *Lutheran Quarterly*, 20:3 (2006): 303–17, showing how E. P. Sanders has in certain regards misread Luther's understanding of Justification.

[7] N. T. Wright, *Justification: God's Plan and Paul's Vision* (London: SPCK, 2009).

essentially an eschatological term. It refers to the hope that God will one day vindicate his people and put things right, and also the way in which he will do this. The 'righteousness of God' (which, of course, is the phrase Luther pondered over for his Reformation breakthrough) means God's faithfulness to his promise to keep his covenant with Israel. When God's righteousness is said to be 'revealed' it simply means that God has after all been faithful to his covenant.

2. *Works of the law as cultural marks of the people of God*: When Paul writes of 'works of the law' he does not mean 'good works' that might earn our way to heaven. Rather, he means the covenantal signs that marked off Israel from the Gentiles. These would, of course, include circumcision, the food laws, laws of cleanliness and washing, the Sabbath and so on. A key question at the heart of Paul's argument in Galatians therefore is not the supposedly Lutheran one of 'how can I find a gracious God?' or 'how can I get to heaven?', but 'how can Jew and Gentile live together in the same church?' The question concerns who is in the covenant and on what basis?

3. *The basis of salvation in Christ*: As a result of this view of the law, the nature of salvation becomes clearer: it is found through faith in Christ as opposed to any cultural or ethnic markers. Faith in Christ is thus the true mark of the one who is justified rather than observance of the Jewish law.

4. *The gospel centres around the Lordship of Christ*: The gospel is at its heart not the offer of the forgiveness of sins, or an invitation to eternal life in heaven with God, but an announcement that Jesus of Nazareth has been raised from the dead, has thus been vindicated as Israel's messiah and is therefore the Lord of the whole world. The Kingdom of God, or the Lordship of Christ, is therefore central to the gospel itself.

Luther and New Perspective Distinctives

In what follows, I try to show how Luther echoes all these insights in his understanding of salvation.

Eschatological Justification

Luther is often thought to have seen justification as forensic, in other words, as a legal fiction where God counts the believer as righteous because of the righteousness of Christ, although in fact he is unrighteous and sinful.[8] As we have seen, Luther's gospel centres on an 'alien righteousness' – a righteousness that is not our own, but that of Christ, which is given to us in faith, and which in turn justifies us.[9] We are justified not by any goodness or holiness inherent in us, however much aided by grace, but instead by the merits and goodness of Christ imputed to us. This can sometimes give the impression that Luther believed justification was a kind of deal, where God decides to ignore the reality of our sin because we have now been clothed with Christ's own righteousness.

However, an exclusively forensic understanding of justification is a position much more clearly found in Melanchthon and later Lutheranism than in Luther himself.[10] Mark Seifrid shows how Luther understands faith as both containing and bringing Christ in with it, whereas Melanchthon sees faith as merely the instrument by which Christ comes separately.[11] For Luther, faith did not so much trigger a transaction by which God gives the righteousness of Christ as merely external imputation, but rather in faith, Christ himself is given, and the believer is united to Christ through faith. Faith 'unites the soul with Christ as a bride is united with her bridegroom'.[12] This explains why Melanchthon has to have a much larger place for a separate doctrine of sanctification than Luther does. Melanchthon narrows the meaning of justification to one image: the legal one of forensic acquittal,

---

[8]This is the view E. P. Sanders seems to attribute to Luther: see E. P. Sanders, *Paul and Palestinian Judaism* (London: SCM, 1977), p. 492, n. 57.

[9]E.g. 'we must be taught a righteousness that comes completely from the outside and is foreign'. *LW* 25.136.

[10]'By 1534, Melanchthon had narrowed the metaphors for justification to a single one: forensic justification.' Timothy J. Wengert, *Law and Gospel: Philip Melanchthon's Debate with John Agricola of Eisleben Over Poenitentia* (Grand Rapids: Baker, 1997), p. 179.

[11]Mark A. Seifrid, 'Luther, Melanchthon and Paul on the Question of Imputation', in Mark Husbands and Daniel J. Treier (eds), *Justification: What's at Stake in the Current Debates* (Downers Grove: Intervarsity Press, 2004), pp. 137–52.

[12]*LW* 31.351.

whereas for Luther, as most Luther scholars now acknowledge, it was a much richer term.[13] The Finnish School of Lutheran interpretation probably overemphasized the extent to which Luther thought Christ himself is conveyed to the believer so that a kind of *theosis* takes place, similar to that in eastern Orthodox soteriology. However, they are onto something: Luther did believe that in faith we participate in Christ himself and all that is his becomes ours.[14] Luther's Christology and his insistence on the Real Presence in the Lord's Supper also tend in the same direction: it is vital that the whole Christ, in both his divine and his human natures, truly and physically becomes ours and we participate in him (rather than a merely external legal transaction) if justification is to be effective.

In particular, Luther clearly understood justification in eschatological terms. It was the anticipation in the present of the final judgement of God on a person. Justification brings forward God's final resolution, his setting things right into the present, so that the believer can foresee that judgement and be sure of it now. At the same time, justification effects the change to which it points forward. In a passage in the Romans commentary of 1515–16, Luther sets out this anticipatory understanding of justification:

> It is similar to the case of a sick man who believes the doctor who promises him a sure recovery and in the meantime obeys the doctor's order in the hope of the promised recovery and abstains from those things which have been forbidden him, so that he may in no way hinder the promised return to health or increase his sickness until the doctor can fulfill his promise to him. Now is this sick man well? The fact is that he is both sick and well at the same time. He is sick in fact, but he is well because of the sure promise of the doctor, whom he trusts and who has reckoned him as already cured, because he is sure that he will cure him; for he has already begun to cure him and no longer reckons to him a sickness unto death. In the same way Christ, our Samaritan, has brought this half-dead man into the inn to be cared for, and he

---

[13]See, e.g. Bernard Lohse, *Martin Luther's Theology: Its Historical and Systematic Development* (Minneapolis: Fortress Press, 1999), pp. 262–6.
[14]Carl E. Braaten and Robert W. Jenson (eds), *Union with Christ: The New Finnish Interpretation of Luther* (Grand Rapids: Wm. B. Eerdmans, 1998).

has begun to heal him, having promised him the most complete cure unto eternal life, and he does not impute his sins, that is, his wicked desires, unto death, but in the meantime in the hope of the promised recovery he prohibits him from doing or omitting things by which his cure might be impeded and his sin, that is, his concupiscence, might be increased. Now, is he perfectly righteous? No, for he is at the same time both a sinner and a righteous man; a sinner in fact, but a righteous man by the sure imputation and promise of God that He will continue to deliver him from sin until He has completely cured him. And thus he is entirely healthy in hope.[15]

This explains the true meaning of Luther's famous '*simul iustus et peccator*'. This is neither a meaningless paradox, nor simply an assertion of God's determination to avoid the tricky issue of sin. It is a statement of Luther's eschatological understanding of Justification: God bringing forward to the present the judgement he will one day bring about. E. P. Sanders writes: 'Those who believe belong to the Lord and become one with him, and in virtue of their incorporation in the Lord, they will be saved on the Day of the Lord.'[16] It could have been written by Luther himself.

Now, of course, Luther refers this primarily to the justification of the individual rather than to the whole cosmos as Paul does (at least as N. T. Wright understands him). However, it is not surprising that this is Luther's focus. The focus on the individual was a factor of Western culture common to both medieval and Renaissance discussions of soteriology. It was the key question of the time, and Luther was simply seeking a Pauline answer to the specific question of individual justification, and he came up with an answer strikingly similar to the understanding of justification we find in many NP scholars: an anticipation in the present of God's final judgement.[17]

---

[15]*LW* 25.260.

[16]Sanders, *Paul and Palestinian Judaism*, p. 523.

[17]Echoing Karl Holl, Alister McGrath explains that for Luther 'God's present justification of the sinner is based upon his anticipation of his final sanctification, in that man's present justification takes place on the basis of his foreseen future righteousness.' Alister E. McGrath, *Iustitia Dei: A History of the Christian Doctrine of Justification* (Cambridge: Cambridge University Press, 1998), p. 198.

Works of the Law as Cultural Markers

Luther is often understood to have aimed his central critique of the medieval church at the idea that good works can earn our way to heaven, or justify us before God. Paul, on the other hand, as far as N. T. Wright and James Dunn see it, was concerned not with good works in that sense, but with Jewish cultural signs, the ethnic practices that marked off the Jews from the Gentiles. Again, on deeper inspection, this is a misrepresentation of both medieval soteriology and Luther's polemics.

First, despite many popular Protestant prejudices, no late medieval theologian taught 'justification by works' in the sense that humans could somehow earn their way to God by their good deeds. All of them, without exception, asserted the necessity of God's grace for salvation. The question was how God's grace interacted with human response. Some at the more Augustinian end of the scale, such as Thomas Bradwardine (c. 1290–1349) or Gregory of Rimini (c. 1300–1358), argued that we could do nothing, as all was basically predestined. Those at the other end of the scale, such as Gabriel Biel, argued that we could perform good works without the help of grace. However, he was keen to add that those works only accrued merit *de congruo*. In other words, they were only of any value because God's covenant decreed they were. Despite being of no value in themselves, he deemed them deserving of the gift of grace. This was the essential presupposition for the ability to perform good works *de condigno*, in other words, works truly deserving of merit. In other words, even this most Pelagian of medieval theologians still asserted the necessity of God's grace and mercy for the performance of good works.

So Luther's target was not the idea that we could somehow earn our way to heaven. The question at stake was how much humans could prepare for grace, what they could do to be justified, or to put it differently, what were the signs of someone in the right with God? Biel was confident that sinners did have to do something – to do what lay within them (*quod in se est*). There were various positions on how much sinners had to contribute to their own salvation, but it was always a contribution – not the whole thing.

Luther's early struggles focused at least in part on his concern that he might not be numbered among the elect people of God. His Romans commentary of 1515–16 returns repeatedly to this theme, of 'he who is overly fearful that he is not elect or is tested concerning his election'[18] or 'those who are anxious and curious about the predestination of themselves or of others'.[19] What if in the secret counsels of God he was in fact among the damned? Luther often seems to have struggled over the issue of predestination, and concluded eventually that such speculation got him (or anyone else for that matter) nowhere.[20] His repeated fears that God would damn him, within the context of late medieval Augustinian understandings of predestination, have to be seen as an anxiety that he had been secretly decreed as outside the grace of God. Luther's fear relates directly to the question of who is among the elect people of God and how it might be possible to tell.

Luther's early training in theology at Erfurt was within the late medieval nominalism mentioned above, with its covenantal understanding of justification, as described in Biel's textbook on the mass, *Sacri canonis missae expositio* of 1499, which Luther read in preparation for his ordination. This view places justification firmly within a covenantal framework. God has established a covenant whereby those who 'do what lies within them' (*facere quod in se est*) are granted grace to perform meritorious works. So, for the early Luther, the question of salvation was precisely: 'What must I do to be within the covenant?' How can I be sure that I have performed the acts recognizable among those who are included within God's covenant?

A key question therefore is what Luther meant by 'works'. To take a set of fairly random examples from one of Luther's commentaries, on the gospel of John, for example, we see him describing 'works' in a very specific way. In his comment on John 3:20, he writes: 'But when it comes to the point that our good works are thereby rejected and counted for nothing and they are told: "You monks must believe this Christ and be saved through Him alone, not through your Masses, pilgrimages, or other ceremonies," then the fight is on; then they call all this nothing but damned heresy.'[21]

---

[18]*LW* 25.377.
[19]*LW* 25.387.
[20]E.g. in the Table Talk, *LW* 54.385: 'I was troubled … by the thought of what God would do with me, but at length I repudiated such a thought and threw myself entirely on his revealed will.'
[21]*LW* 22.370.

On John 16:4, he says:

For what they say with their mouths about God, Christ, His Baptism, etc., they deny with their whole being and with their works – monasticism, Masses, indulgences, adoration of the saints, etc. Therefore it is all a futile and condemned worship of God.[22]

And on John 14:15:

Yes, instead of becoming acquainted with God through Christ, we made the dear Savior a Judge and ran from Him to the Virgin Mary and other saints as intercessors and mediators. We also sought reconciliation by means of our works, Masses, monastic life, fasting, and prayer. These are the very thoughts that lead away from this article and prevent it from being understood and applied. One may refer to and discuss it superficially, but this is like a blind man's discussion of color.[23]

The point is clear: when Luther uses the word 'works' he commonly meant not so much moral works of goodness (although, to be fair, these were included within the definition), but primarily cultic religious acts, ceremonies that had become the cultural markers of the late medieval Christian. 'Works' were most often masses, pilgrimages, devotions, prayers, satisfactions and the like. Of course, the whole Reformation was sparked by his outrage at the dependence for salvation not on moral good deeds, but on a specific religious and cultural practice of the late middle ages: Indulgences. The 95 Theses are a diatribe against reliance on cultural and cultic acts as the sign of the truly righteous, or the elect.

Luther's point was that cultural markers such as masses, pilgrimages, indulgences and confessions were not the true sign of the one who was justified, or to put it in the language of the nominalist soteriology in which he was taught, within the covenant of God: the only true sign was faith in Christ. Paul's point, according to Wright and Dunn, is that circumcision, food laws, keeping the Sabbath and washings are not the true sign of the one who is justified or to put

---

[22] *LW* 24.328.
[23] *LW* 24.98.

it in the language of first-century Judaism, within the covenant people of God: the only true sign was faith in Christ. The positions are remarkably similar in structure, even if different in expression. It is basically the same idea applied in different contexts.

The Basis of Salvation in Christ

As Luther put it in Thesis 25 of the Heidelberg Disputation of 1518: 'He is not righteous who does much, but he who, without work, believes much in Christ.'[24] This brings us to the key point of convergence. Paul and Luther were clearly writing in very different times and cultural contexts, yet their description of salvation is almost identical. According to Wright, Paul argues that since the life, death and resurrection of Christ, a new age has dawned. Now salvation comes not through observance of the law, through ethnic belonging to the race of Israel with its temple, circumcision, food laws and so on, but by faith in Christ, and Christ alone. This meant the scandalous teaching (to Jewish ears) that Gentiles whose faith was in Christ could be counted as being within the covenant people of God without having to become Jews, and the foolish idea (to Greeks) that salvation came through a crucified Jewish Messiah.

Luther's central insistence was exactly the same in a different context. He was clearly not writing to define the status of Jew and Gentile within the new covenant, but he was still eager to define what was the basis of membership of God's people, what was the sign of the elect, the truly righteous, and his answer was the same as Paul's: faith in Jesus, the crucified messiah.

For Luther Christology was at the very heart of theology and soteriology. God was revealed in Christ, and salvation consisted in the gift of Christ alone. This is Luther's gospel – that we are justified by the merits of another – Christ himself. His insistence on 'faith alone' can give the impression that it is the act of faith that justifies. However, it is clear that it is faith in *Christ* that justifies: 'However, we need to be certain, and so God in his grace has provided us with a Man in whom we may trust, rather than in our works. For although he has justified us through the gift of faith, and although he becomes favorable to us through his grace, yet he wants us to

---

[24]*LW* 31.55.

rely on Christ so that we will not waver in ourselves and in these his gifts, nor be satisfied with the righteousness which has begun in us unless it cleaves to and flows from Christ's righteousness.'[25] In this sense, 'Justification by Faith' is a misleading phrase if it is taken to mean that we are justified by the power of our faith. Nothing could be further from Luther's mind. We are instead justified when Christ and his righteousness become ours, and they become ours when received by faith. Faith in this transaction is instrumental, not causative. It is not the cause of Justification, but only the means by which it is received. In faith, Christ and his righteousness become ours and thus we are justified. Any suggestion that anything else but Christ can justify is to be strongly resisted.

Luther's controversial insistence on 'faith alone' has sometimes been criticized as going beyond St Paul, particularly as he adds the word 'alone' in his translation of Paul in Romans 3:28, as we saw in the last chapter. However, clearly both say effectively the same thing. In Galatians, Paul argues that salvation comes through faith in Christ alone, not through faith in Christ allied to circumcision. Luther argues that salvation comes through faith in Christ alone, not faith allied to pilgrimages, masses and relics. Neither Paul nor Luther compromise on the centrality of Christ to Christian soteriology and theology. 'Christ alone' could, in fact, be a watchword for both.

The Lordship of Christ

N. T. Wright insists that the central message of Paul and indeed the whole of the NT, is the Lordship of Christ: 'If Jesus is Israel's messiah, then he is the world's true Lord.'[26] This seems at first sight to be fundamentally different from Luther's insistence on the centrality of Justification by Faith, the 'article by which the church stands or falls'. Luther seems to place justification, forgiveness, the individual and imputation of righteousness at the heart, whereas Paul places the Lordship of Christ at the centre.

It is not quite as simple as this, however. In 1947, Philip Watson published what became a significant book in Luther scholarship,

---

[25] LW 32.235.
[26] N. T. Wright, *Paul: Fresh Perspectives* (London: SPCK, 2005), p. 69.

titled *Let God Be God! An Interpretation of the Theology of Martin Luther*.[27] The book emphasized the theocentricity of Luther's theology: that it was in essence an appeal to 'let God be God'. Rather than an anthropocentric view of life that placed humankind at the centre, Luther's was a theology that radically redrew the world, with God at the centre as the world's true Lord, and humankind in its proper place as part of creation. For Luther, the first commandment, to love God with all our heart, soul, mind and strength is the heart of true religion and the epicentre of the human calling. And this commandment is fulfilled through faith: 'The First Commandment ... is fulfilled by faith alone.'[28] Faith recognizes God as God and Christ as the true Lord. To trust in human works is to glorify ourselves to place our own activity and action at the centre of the picture: it is to 'utterly take from him the glory of his divinity'. To 'let be God be God' means to recognize him in Christ. And to trust in Christ is to acknowledge his true place as the giver of all good things. Faith alone honours God, trusts him and takes him at his word.

The doctrine of Justification by Faith is therefore for Luther an acknowledgement of the divinity of God and the Lordship of Christ over the world. It is an obedience that recognizes the Lordship of Christ over the sinner and over the world. It is letting God be God and an acknowledgement of the centrality of Christ to all of life.

Conclusion

Luther's theology is perhaps best seen as an interpretation of Pauline theology for the fast-changing world of sixteenth-century Europe. In the hands of a spiritual and theological genius such as Luther, Paul's theology proved rich and fertile enough to speak powerfully to the questions and concerns of Europeans in this century as it was to do through John Wesley in the eighteenth, Karl Barth in the twentieth and the New Perspective in the twenty-first. And Luther's was a remarkably faithful interpretation of Paul. At its heart were the vital themes of God's gracious judgement in the future, brought into

---

[27]Philip S. Watson, *Let God Be God! An Interpretation of the Theology of Martin Luther* (London: Epworth, 1947).
[28]*LW* 31.353.

the present, the instrumentality of faith, salvation through Christ alone, and the call to obedience to Christ as God's Son and self-revelation. It had a different feel and altered emphases from Paul's own theology, but that is hardly to be wondered at, given the differences between the first-century Greco-Roman world and sixteenth-century Germany. Rather than pitting Paul against Luther, at least some parts of the NP might need to recognize Luther as a faithful interpreter of Paul after all.

PART B

Luther in His Time

4

Luther on the Death
of Christ

Historiographically, Martin Luther is enigmatic. Does he belong to the past or to the future? Was he one of the last blasts of medieval sentiment, full of superstitious belief in devils and angels, quaintly preoccupied with the vestiges of a fading cultural order? Or should he be viewed as one of the main prophets or precursors of the modern age?

Protestant historians and theologians have tended to paint him as the latter, a harbinger of a new era and bold pioneer of the modern world. In doing so, they tended to emphasize the extent to which he broke from the medieval past, leaving behind the credulity of a primitive age, crafting a religion much better suited for modernity whether in its rationalist or religious forms.

However, constructing the debate in such a dichotomous way risks obscuring, rather than illuminating, the nuances of Luther and his theology. Luther must necessarily be understood both as someone who, inevitably, shared the characteristics of his own age and as a figure who shaped subsequent centuries in ways neither he nor any of his contemporaries could have imagined.

One example of this is found in one key idea in the early Luther: his Theology of the Cross. The development of the idea against the background of late medieval theology has been well described by Alister McGrath.[1] He argues that the *theologia crucis* was the theological method that, when applied to the issue

---

[1] Alister E. McGrath, *Luther's Theology of the Cross* (Oxford: Blackwell, 1985).

of justification, produced the Reformation breakthrough, and the gospel of Christ's alien righteousness that becomes ours by faith, and shows convincingly the strong links between the *theologia crucis* and the subsequent theology of Justification by Faith. From this perspective, the Theology of the Cross is seen largely as a reaction against the soteriology of the *via moderna*, the theological tradition in which Luther was trained in the University of Erfurt, and a critique of late medieval scholasticism. McGrath interprets this theology primarily as a *repudiation* of elements in the late medieval scene. Walter Von Loewenich's earlier study confined itself to an account of how the theme developed within Luther's own writings from the Heidelberg Disputation of 1518 onwards, a description and analysis of that theology, including a section on the influence of mysticism on the younger Luther. He mentions (only to refute) the older thesis that Luther's Ockhamism explains his *theologia crucis*,[2] but beyond this, not much attention is given to its origins in Luther's background. Although the last and briefest chapter of McGrath's book is titled 'The Origins and Significance of the Theology of the Cross', his real interest lies in the relationship between this doctrine and the Reformation breakthrough, and Luther's intellectual background in the *via moderna*, so there is little reflection on the sources of the doctrine other than this. The book describes the 'winds of doctrine' against which Luther's Theology of the Cross was struggling (i.e. Aristotelian scholasticism and the *via moderna*), but not the soil out of which it grew.

The approach that sees Luther's *theologia crucis* as a break from the late medieval theological tradition, while valid up to a point, is potentially misleading if taken on its own, where it might suggest that Luther's *theologia crucis* was purely a repudiation of late medieval Catholicism. It needs to be balanced by a different perspective, namely, that the reformer's *theologia crucis* was at the same time a reassertion of other important elements within that late medieval context. The *theologia crucis*, the idea that the cross of Christ is of critical importance for spirituality and for understanding the nature of God, was kept alive in aspects of popular devotion, apart from the controlling paradigms of theology, before Luther appropriated

---

[2]Walter Von Loewenich, *Luther's Theology of the Cross* (Belfast: Christian Journals, 1976), pp. 65–77.

it into theological discourse. In fact, this chapter argues that it helped resolve Luther's growing awareness of a fundamental contradiction between his own spiritual and theological origins, a dissonance between late medieval spirituality and theology that cried out for resolution.

Walter Von Loewenich suggested five hallmarks of Luther's Theology of the Cross, which can function as a working definition of the doctrine:

1. The Theology of the Cross is a theology of revelation, as opposed to speculation.
2. God's revelation is indirect and concealed.
3. This revelation is recognized in suffering not in works.
4. The God hidden in his revelation is known only by faith.
5. God is known in the 'practical thought of suffering'.[3]

Where did Luther get these insights from? A glance at three early writings from Luther helps us appreciate both Luther's own debt to medieval piety and the nature of his early theological development.

Luther and Late Medieval Passion Meditation

Contemplation on the sufferings of Christ was the heart of late medieval piety, not least within the Augustinian order, of which Luther was a member. Such contemplation took a wide variety of forms: meditations, prayers, imagined conversations between Christ and his mother in Bethany, some retelling the story of the passion, some using OT figures, some printed, some handwritten. Popular and monastic piety, both of which Luther would have known from his earliest days, were steeped in such meditation. This tradition has been described by Martin Elze,[4] and on a wider canvas

---

[3]Ibid., p. 22; McGrath produces a similar list, *Luther's Theology*, pp. 149–50.

[4]Martin Elze, 'Das Verständnis der Passion Jesu im Ausgehenden Mittelalter und bei Luther', in Kurt Aland, Walther Eltester, Heinz Liebling and Klaus Scholder (eds), *Geist und Geschichte der Reformation* (Festgabe H. Rückert; Berlin: Walter de Gruyter, 1966), pp. 127–51.

by Berndt Hamm, who divides it into two types:[5] The first, which he calls 'the Outer Way', and which counters late medieval insecurity by directing the would-be penitent to the objective guarantees of the sacramental life of the Church, is represented by Johannes von Paltz, who shared the Augustinian monastery at Erfurt with Luther for two years before moving on to become prior of Mühlheim in 1507, and is also found in some of Luther's later opponents such as Johannes Tetzel, Conrad Wimpina and Sylvester Prierias. The other, 'the Inner Way', is represented by Johannes von Staupitz, Johannes Lang, Andreas Karlstadt, Wenceslaus Linck, Spengler and even at times, as we shall see, although in a different way, Luther himself. It focuses less on the objective guarantees of the institutional church, and more on the subjective relationship of the individual soul to Christ.

Luther seems to have been especially conscious of this varied tradition and practice in the period 1517–19, as can be shown by reference to a number of works in that period, to which we now turn.

1. *Sermon von der Betrachtung des heyligen leydens Christi*: Luther gives striking confirmation of the existence of these two types of meditation on the cross in this piece, planned towards the end of his lectures on Galatians, and finally published on 5 April 1519.[6] Luther shows that he has experienced these lengthy lugubrious meditations and perhaps even dozed off during them. The introductory paragraphs of the work refer to the benefits claimed by many in meditating on Christ's passion, and to those who 'feel pity for Christ, lamenting and bewailing his innocence'. Luther caustically compares them to the women rebuked by Christ on the way to the cross, whom Christ instructs not to weep for him but for themselves. This description naturally fits what Hamm calls 'the Inner way', especially in its orientation to inner compassion for the sufferings of Christ.

Luther proceeds to speak of another type of meditation: that of those 'who have learned what rich fruits the holy mass offers. In their simple-mindedness they think it enough simply to hear mass.

---

[5]Berndt Hamm, *Frömmigkeit Am Anfang Des 16. Jahrhunderts: Studien Zu Johannes Von Paltz Und Seinem Umkreis* (Tübingen: Mohr, 1982), pp. 222–47.
[6]WA 2.136–42. See Luther's letter to Spalatin (13 March 1519) in *WA BR*, 1.359–60, which indicates the importance of this work for Luther, given his need to make time to plan and write it out during a very busy writing and lecturing schedule.

In support of this several teachers are cited to us who hold that the mass is *opere operati, non opere operantis'*. Luther rejects the view that the mass is an end in itself, but instead points to its reference to the cross of Christ. Given Hamm's description of 'the Outer Way', which aimed to direct people to the efficacy of the sacraments in general and the mass in particular, Luther's point becomes clear. In this common type of meditation, the cross of Christ was intended to direct sinners to the mass. For Luther, this is to get it the wrong way round – the mass is to direct them to the cross of Christ.[7]

2. *Hebrews commentary*: Luther's own view of the value of meditation on the passion of Christ can be glimpsed in a comment made on Hebrews 9:14 towards the end of his lectures on that book given between April 1517 and March 1518: 'Those who meditate on Christ's Passion only in order that they may suffer with him or gain from it something else than faith meditate in a way that is nothing short of fruitless and heathenish ... But one should think of his Passion with the desire that faith should be increased, namely that the more frequently one meditates, the more fully one believes that the blood of Christ was shed for one's own sins.'[8] This is clearly both a criticism of contemporary styles of passion meditation and, at the same time, a commendation of the practice, when carried out with the right aim in mind. Luther criticizes meditating on the cross with the purpose of inspiring inner *compassio* with the sufferings of Christ. Both this type of passion meditation and, by implication, that aimed at directing the sinner to the sacraments of the Church are condemned as misguided. The only worthwhile aim of meditation on the passion is faith, in other words, believing that one's own sins are forgiven by Christ through the cross.

3. *Good Friday Sermons 1518*: Luther also handles the subject of passion meditation in two sermons dated by the editors of the Weimar Edition as preached on Good Friday, 1518.[9] These initially strike a more positive note, praising passion meditation as very beneficial. While valuing the practice, Luther is keen to direct the sinner to meditation that is properly fruitful. The first sermon stresses the idea that the cross was 'for us', the importance of grasping the idea that the sufferings of Christ were undergone for the sake of the

---

[7]*'umb des leydens Christi willen zu bedenken'*, WA 2.137.3–4.
[8]WA 57.209.16–21; LW 29.210–11.
[9]'Duo sermones de passione Christi', WA 1.335–45.

Christian. Conformity to Christ is the main aim of passion meditation, yet this is understood in a wholly different way from most late medieval passion meditation. Instead of inner compassion/sympathy for Christ and outer imitation of his sufferings, Luther urges a concern for one's own sins, which led Christ to the cross. The sinner is to weep not for Christ, but for himself. It is vital to see oneself in the suffering of Christ on the cross, as one meditates on it. The art of passion meditation according to Luther is 'reading oneself in Christ',[10] an art that, he argues, typical late medieval meditation missed altogether. The second of these sermons makes similar points, stressing the necessity of gratitude for the death of Christ 'for us', and that Christ's death is to be seen as much more than an example to be followed.

Martin Elze has examined these two sermons to indicate Luther's divergence from late medieval patterns of meditation on the cross.[11] He stresses Luther's use of the Augustinian distinction between the cross as *exemplum* and as *sacramentum (mysterium)*.[12] This, he argues, is the major difference between Luther and traditional ways of meditating on the passion. Luther stresses Christ's suffering as not just an example to be followed, but also something undertaken by Christ *pro se*, bringing the sinner to a new self-knowledge before God, that is, to faith.[13] Martin Nicol has also studied these sermons, yet disagrees with Elze on Luther's rejection of *compassio*.[14] Nicol suggests that Luther picks up this element and reworks it: for Luther, the meditator is to engage not just with Christ's sufferings, but also with the effect of her own sins in the cross of Christ, and the love of God shown in the cross. The process is to lead not to mystical union with Christ, but to a proper *imitatio* in the sense of the shared experience of *Anfechtung*.

Close examination of the second sermon both confirms and develops Nicol's argument. The distinction Luther makes there is different from the typical *affectus/effectus* (i.e. inner and outer)

---

[10]'*se ipsum in Christo legens*', WA 1.338.35.

[11]Elze, 'Das Verständnis der Passion Jesu', part II.

[12]WA 1.339.17–19. Luther also uses this idea in the lectures on Galatians: cf. WA 2.501.34–7.

[13]Elze, 'Das Verständnis der Passion Jesu', p. 144.

[14]Martin Nicol, *Meditation bei Luther* (Forschungen zur Kirchen- und Dogmengeschichte, 34; Göttingen: Vandenhoeck & Ruprecht, 1984), pp. 117–50.

distinction in such works of piety. Luther actually contrasts the *affectus* not with the *effectus*, but with the *intellectus*.[15] Luther's point is to urge inner compassion for Christ not as opposed to outer imitation, but as opposed to dry intellectual analysis. There needs to be an emotional engagement with Christ's sufferings, namely, feeling the effect on Christ of the judgement of one's sins.[16] Luther commends passion meditation precisely because it engages the emotions and not just the intellect. Here Luther commends part of the Inner Way, not because it can foster a feeling of sorrow and sympathy for Christ, but rather because it can stimulate an awareness of sorrow for one's own sins, which goes beyond dry intellectual recognition. Nicol's recognition of the importance of the emotional engagement with the passion is entirely correct. However, Luther develops this point as a polemical device against forms of theology and spirituality, which would limit the engagement to the intellectual sphere: it becomes a critique of intellectualized scholastic theology as well as of late medieval patterns of passion meditation. Luther has used this standard form of late medieval spirituality, and developed it in such a way as to turn it against the theology of the Scholastics.

Returning to Luther's 1519 *Sermon von der Betrachtung des heyligen leydens Christi*, it displays again both his dependence on contemporary types of passion meditation and, at the same time, his independence from that tradition. Here again, passion meditation is commended, its emotional impact approved and the concept of the cross as *sacramentum* employed. Its first aim is self-knowledge, that 'man sees into his own true self and that he be terrified and crushed by this'.[17] The cross reminds the observer of how much his sin has caused Christ to suffer, and so he is led to despair of himself. True meditation on the death of Christ lays the blame for the cross squarely at one's own feet. False meditation seeks to lay the blame

---

[15]'*Scriptura quoque nos hortatur magis ad affectum passionis Christi quam intellectum.*' WA 1.343.28–9. '*Ideoque intellectus non potest capere nec lingua dicere nec littera scribere, sed tantum affectus percipere, quid sit Christum passum esse: omina enim absorbet infinitum.*' WA 1.344.9–11.

[16]WA 1.343.4–12. Luther here uses the picture of the women weeping for Christ on his way to the cross, and his admonition to them to weep not for him, but for themselves. This image is used in the 1519 Sermon on the Meditation of Christ's Passion: the thought expressed in both is similar.

[17]WA 2.138.15–19.

for it elsewhere, on either Judas or the Jews.[18] True meditation suffers the pain of knowing that one's own sins have crucified Christ. False meditation seeks to avoid suffering by carrying the cross as a charm,[19] simply generating fruitless pity for Christ or thinking it enough to go to hear mass.[20]

Having seen the effect of his own sin on Christ, the meditator is then to pass from Good Friday to Easter Sunday, and believe not just that 'sin cannot remain on Christ since it is swallowed up by his resurrection',[21] but also that 'his wounds and sufferings are your sins, to be borne and paid by him'.[22] This promise must be clung to despite the sting of conscience,[23] and proves to be more effective in bringing peace of conscience than any amount of contrition and penance.[24] Having believed this, the meditator is to take Christ's passion from then on as a 'pattern for your entire life ... Until now we regarded it as a sacrament which is active in us while we are passive, but now we find that we too must be active'.[25]

We can now begin to summarize Luther's own attitude to meditation on the passion of Christ in relation to common late medieval practise.

1. Luther commends the common practise of meditation on the passion of Christ as spiritually beneficial, because it centres on the cross as the heart of Christian faith, and because it engages not just the *intellectus*, but also the *affectus*. This is continuous with common practise in urging an emotional engagement with Christ's sufferings, as in what Berndt Hamm called 'the Inner Way'.

2. As Elze points out, Luther employs Augustine's concept of the cross as *sacramentum*, not just as *exemplum*, to advance beyond the traditional pattern of passion meditation. In this,

---

[18] *WA* 2.136.3–10.
[19] *WA* 2.136.15–20.
[20] *WA* 2.136.21–137.9.
[21] *WA* 2.140.18–19.
[22] 'das seyne wunden und leyden seyn deyn sunde, das er sie trage und bezale.' *WA* 2.140.7–8.
[23] 'Auff dise unnd der gleychenn spruch mustu mit gannzem wag dich vorlassen, so vil mehr, so herter dich deynn gewissen martert.' *WA* 2.140.11–13.
[24] 'rewe und gnugthuung', *WA* 2.140.13–15.
[25] *WA* 2.141.11–13.

he at once accepts the objective understanding of the cross as atonement for sins, as in 'the Outer Way', yet goes beyond it in denying that this is channelled only through sacramental and institutional practise.

3. Meditation on the passion is instead directly related to faith, that is, believing the promise that Christ's sufferings were effective in dealing with sin, and done 'for us'.

4. Luther's critique of current practise concerns its mistaken focus. When such meditation fails to lead to sorrow for sin, it is pointless. For Luther, much of the late medieval practice of passion meditation leads only to laying the blame on others, avoiding suffering, fostering a sentimental pity for Christ or a misplaced trust in the mass as automatically effective.

5. Besides a critique of current practise in passion meditation, he develops a critique of unengaged, intellectualized scholastic theology that fails to grasp the depths of the cross at an emotional or affective level.

6. Luther therefore quite clearly shows both continuity and discontinuity (at least by about 1518) from the main strands of meditation on the cross in operation in his time. Luther rejects some elements of the traditional practice. He is drawn to passion meditation neither as an impulse to subjective inner *compassio* for Christ nor as a commendation of the objective efficacy of the sacraments. Yet he takes up other aspects of the tradition, namely, the need for emotional engagement and a sense of the objectivity of what Christ has achieved on the cross. These, however, emerge reconfigured and reworked. An emotional response is directed not to sorrow for Christ, but to sorrow for oneself, and the objective work of Christ leads not to the sacraments but to meditation on and thankfulness for God's love and forgiveness.

In such passion meditation and Luther's response to it, we can trace several of the themes of the emerging *theologia crucis*: the value of suffering, the preference for experience over speculation (*affectus* over *intellectus*), the need for sinners to see themselves in the suffering of Christ, the immediate link with faith as the appropriate mode of knowledge of God, the opposition of suffering to works of contrition or penance, the work of the cross as bringing the sinner to despair over his own sins. It is surely significant that the period in which Luther ponders repeatedly on passion meditation coincides exactly with the period leading up to the Heidelberg Disputation, in which the *theologia crucis* receives its sharpest exposition. If Luther's comment in the lectures on Hebrews was written in the winter of 1517–18, the *Duo sermones de passione Christi* were preached on 2 April 1518, and Luther set out on foot for Heidelberg exactly a week later, they clearly emerge from the same frame of mind. Again, the 'Meditation on Christ's Passion' was published on 5 April 1519, while the first part of Luther's second set of lectures on the Psalms, a work pervaded by the Theology of the Cross, appeared a week later on 13 April 1519.[26]

This common feature of late medieval piety, with which Luther was clearly familiar from an early date, provided him with both a passion-centred spirituality, reminded him of the significance of the cross as providing effective satisfaction for sins and the importance of emotional, not merely speculative engagement with the passion of Christ. As is common with Luther's use of his sources, he goes well beyond current practice and aims to reform it in line with his own emerging theology. Yet he quite clearly recommends reform rather than rejection. In the emergence of the Theology of the Cross, late medieval passion meditation plays a significant role. Yet there is at least one other source of this theology, to which we now turn.

Luther and Bernard of Clairvaux

The only medieval author quoted with approval in Luther's 1519 'Meditation on Christ's Passion' is Bernard of Clairvaux. Towards the end of the work, he cites Bernard as an example of one who did exactly as he is recommending, namely, allowing the passion to remind him of the effect of his sins on Christ, and thus the judgement hanging over him.[27] Bernard has been seen as 'the true father of Passion Literature of the following three centuries'.[28]

---

[26]The lectures began in the winter of early 1519, and the dedication to the printed edition of the first part is dated 27 March 1519.

[27]WA 2.137.37–9.

[28]KurtRuh, Zur Theologie des Mittelalterlichen Passionstraktats, *Theologische Zeitschrift* 6 (1950): 17–39 (18).

In the monastic piety in which Luther's early years were spent, the figure of Bernard loomed large, and his sermons were one of the most popular texts in that monastic world. Luther had quite probably read Bernard's work while at the monastery in Erfurt,[29] would have heard them read over meals while there and encountered them again through his close study of Biel's *canonis missae expositio*.[30] The influence of Bernard on Luther's early theology has often been noticed. There are, of course, real differences between the thought of the mature Luther and Bernard. After the Leipzig Disputation of 1519, the Reformer used the Cistercian more rarely and with much greater caution, making a clear distinction between Bernard's personal piety, which he still found exemplary, and his theology, which he did not. However, the *young* Luther found Bernard's writing more congenial, in particular, the connections between Bernard and the emerging Theology of the Cross. The extent of Bernard's influence on the origins of the Theology of the Cross can be seen through a study of the main outlines of Bernard's teaching on the cross and humility, particularly in the work from which Luther quotes most often, Bernard's sermons on the Song of Songs.[31]

1. *Luther and Bernard's sermons on the Song of Songs*: Like Luther, Bernard echoes Augustine's combination of the cross as both *sacramentum* and *exemplum*: 'He is yet not one who only forgives, but even offers himself as an example to follow. Hence as you well know, these sentiments are often on my lips, and God knows they

---

[29]The Erfurt friary had a copy of the 1476–7 Augsburg edition of Bernard's *De consideratione*, as well as his sermons on the Song of Songs and *Sermones de tempore et de sanctis*: see Jun Matsuura, 'Restbestände aus der Bibliothek des Erfurter Augustinerklosters zu Luthers Zeit Und bisher unbekannte eigenhändige Notizen Luthers: Ein Berichte', *Lutheriana: Zum 500. Geburtstag Martin Luthers Von Den Mitarbeitern Der Weimarer Ausgabe* (Archiv zur Weimarer Ausgabe der Werke Martin Luthers, vol. 5; Köln: Böhlau, 1984), pp. 318, 324, 326. Cf. also Theo Bell, *Divus Bernhardus: Bernhard Von Clairvaus in Martin Luthers Schriften* (Veröffentlichungen des Instituts für Europäische Geschichte Mainz, 148; Mainz: P. von Sabern, 1993), p. 28.

[30]Bell, *Divus Bernhardus*, p. 31; Heiko A. Oberman, *The Harvest of Medieval Theology: Gabriel Biel and Late Medieval Nominalism* (Cambridge, MA: Harvard University Press, 1963), pp. 5, 141.

[31]The quotations here are taken from the English translation of the sermons: Bernard of Clairvaux, *The Works of Bernard of Clairvaux*, trans. Killian Walsh (Kalamazoo: Cistercian Publications, 1976). The volume and page numbers are from this edition.

are always in my heart. This is my philosophy, one more refined
and interior, to know Jesus and him crucified.'[32] Meditation on the
cross of Christ is therefore a sure means of consolation in anxiety. Bernard often makes reference to God's mercy hiding behind
his anger: 'It is when God does not show his anger that he is most
angry ... I prefer that you be angry with me, O Father of Mercies.'[33]
In Sermon 61, Bernard combines two images. The first is of the Song
of Solomon 2.14, where following Gregory the Great, he interprets
the dove nesting in a cleft in a rock as the believer resting in the
wounds of Christ (seen as the clefts in the rock, which is Christ
himself). The other image is that of Exodus 33:22–33: 'I shall be as
the dove nesting in the highest point of the cleft, so that like Moses
in his cleft of the rock, I may be able to see at least the back of the
Lord as he passes by. For who can look on his face as he stands, but
he who is introduced not only to the holy place but to the holy of
holies ... This contemplation of him is not to be despised ... One
day he will show his face in its dignity and glory, now let him show
"the back" of his gracious concern. He is great in his kingdom, but
so gentle on the cross.'[34] For Bernard, the 'back' of God is his gentle
love shown on the cross, his 'lowliness' or 'shadow'. His 'front' is
the full majesty of his glory, greatness and splendour. The Christian
is to be satisfied with the vision of God's 'back' in the wounds of
Christ, while for the 'dove', that is, the penitent, 'all her affections
are preoccupied with the wounds of Christ; she abides in them by
constant meditation'.[35]

The Church and the individual Christian[36] are to be conformed
not to Christ's majesty, but to his humility and lowliness: 'She [the
Church] is not overwhelmed by glory because she does not arrogate
it to herself. She is not overwhelmed because she is a scrutinizer not
of God's majesty, but of his will. What touches upon his majesty,
she does indeed sometimes dare to contemplate, but in admiration,
not in scrutiny.'[37] The Church is to concern itself with Christ in his

---

[32]Sermon 43 (III) 4, Vol. II, p. 223.
[33]Sermon 42 (II) 4, Vol. II, p. 213. Cf. also Sermon 23 (V) 14, Vol. II, p. 38 and 23
(VI) 16, Vol. II, p. 40.
[34]Sermon 61 (III) 6, Vol. III, p. 146..
[35]Sermon 61 (III) 7, Vol. III, p. 146.
[36]Sermon 62 (III) 5, Vol. III, p. 156.
[37]Sermon 62 (III) Vol. III, 4, Vol. III, p. 155.

humanity and weakness before his glory, as they provide the essential example of humility to be followed.[38]

Bernard's teaching on humility works within the framework of the Benedictine teaching of the twelve steps.[39] Humility, the virtue that pleases God above all others,[40] is conceived as *'virtus, qua homo verissima sui agnitione sibi ipsi vilescit'*.[41] Indeed 'no-one is saved without self-knowledge, since it is the source of that humility on which salvation depends'.[42] To be humble means accepting not our own image of ourselves, but God's truthful estimate of us.[43] The central picture of humility for Bernard is the crucified Christ.[44]

Sermon 34 specifically deals with the topic of humility. God is like a physician who sends trials and temptations with the express purpose of healing the soul. God brings his grace to the soul by humbling it: 'When you perceive that you are being humbled/humiliated, look on it as the sign of a sure guarantee that grace is on its way. Just as the heart is puffed up with pride before its destruction, so it is humiliated before it is honoured.'[45] Bernard considers the example of David, and the way in which God used his humiliation to work out his real purpose for him: 'While the wicked tongue raged against him, his mind was intent on discovering the hidden purpose of God ... God made use of it [criticism and blasphemy] to humiliate David ... Do you see that humility makes us righteous?'[46] For Bernard, it is strictly speaking humility and not humiliation that 'makes us righteous', in that humiliation must be received, welcomed and embraced gladly if the precious virtue of humility is to follow from it. Humiliation sent by God leads to humility, which in turn leads to the giving of grace.

---

[38]'De Gradibus Humilitatis et Superbiae', in *The Works of Bernard of Clairvaux* (VII) 21, pp. 48–50.

[39]See Rudolf Damerau, *Die Demut in Der Theologie Luthers* (Giessen: Schmitz, 1967), pp. 32–9.

[40]Sermon 42 (VI) 9, Vol. II, p. 218.

[41]'De Gradibus Humilitatis et Superbiae', in Bernard of Clairvaux, *Opera Omnia* (J. P. Migne; Patrologia Cursus Completus Series Latina, 182; Paris, 1879), p. 942. PL 182, 942. English translation (I) 2, p. 30.

[42]*Song of Songs*, Sermon 37 (II), Vol. II, p. 181.

[43]Sermon 37 (III) 6, Vol. II, p. 183.

[44]Sermon 42 (V) 8, Vol. II, p. 216.

[45]Sermon 34. 1, Vol. II, p. 161.

[46]Sermon 34. 2–3, Vol. II, pp. 161–2.

The human soul is able to cooperate with God in this work. The servant of God works along with the Holy Spirit: all that is needed is for the soul to turn, to cry out, to humble itself: 'Every soul, I say, standing thus under condemnation and without hope, has the power to turn and find it can not only breathe the fresh air of the hope of pardon and mercy, but also dare to aspire to the nuptials of the Word.' The soul is to ascend to God by means of humility. Sin, in the form of pride, obscures the original human likeness to God, and the process of salvation is one in which sin and pride are overcome, and the believer grows in likeness to Christ, a hard, but possible path: 'so think of the question "Lord who is like you?" in terms of difficulty, not of impossibility.'[47]

Given Luther's familiarity with Bernard, it is striking how many of these themes coincide with the *theologia crucis*. Bernard perceives the importance of suffering for the Christian, and believes that God deliberately sends it on the Christian to humble him. Luther's distinction between God's 'own work' and his 'alien work' is reflected in Bernard's preference for God's anger. The stress on Christ's humility and lowliness, rather than his glory and power, as the accessible face of God is similar to that of Luther, and perhaps most remarkably, Bernard's use of Exodus 33, the idea of the 'back' of God is a very close parallel to Luther's use of the same passage and idea. Luther never explicitly quotes from this passage in Bernard, although he often quotes Bernard without citing him directly.[48] At this early stage in Luther's thought, he understands the 'back' of God as Christ's humanity, his 'front' as his divinity, in other words, focusing on the incarnation. Bernard, however, sees God's 'back' as the wounds of Christ, focusing on the crucifixion. Such a passage, surely known to Luther, must have focused his thoughts increasingly on God's self-revelation as not merely taking place in the incarnation, but more sharply on the cross itself. Later on, Luther of course used Exodus 33 in Thesis 20 of the Heidelberg Disputation,[49] where the reference has now explicitly moved to the

---

[47]Sermon 82 (III) 7, Vol. IV, p. 179.

[48]Cf. Franz Posset, 'Recommendation by Martin Luther on Saint Bernard's *On Consideration*', *Cistercian Studies* 25:1 (1990): 25–36, for Luther's often uncited use of Bernard's *De Consideratione* in the Romans and Hebrew lectures. See also, e.g. WA 57-3.215.9–10, where the quotation originally comes from Bernard: see *LW* 29.216 n. 26; WA 2.138.13–14 and *LW* 42.10 n. 14.

[49]WA 1.354.19–20.

cross rather than to the incarnation. It is quite possible that it was Bernard's version of the *posteriora dei* that influenced Luther in this direction. At the very least, their use of Exodus 33 is so similar that we can speak of Bernard's conception as displaying the type of meditation on the cross within which Luther also came to develop his understanding of the alien revelation of God.

2. *Luther's use of other Bernardian ideas*: Luther also refers to Bernard's insistence on the need for constant repentance and explicitly attributes to Bernard recognition of two things disregarded by the whole world: the fact that the entire human race is mired in sin and that no one can merit the forgiveness of sins.[50] He notices Bernard's remarks on the difference between God's estimation of things and human perspectives,[51] and his teaching that coming to Christ means despising the good and evil fortunes of this life.[52]

Bernard's threefold analysis of church history[53] crops up frequently in Luther's first Lectures on the Psalms. Luther takes Bernard's idea that the first age was marked by persecutions, the second by heresy, the third by ease and comfort, preceding the imminent end of the age.[54] Luther uses it to point out the danger the church is in, precisely because of the peace and security it enjoys. From this Luther develops the idea that the church is in greatest danger when it is rich, well-fed and powerful, and most blessed when it is poor, persecuted and tempted. Most significantly, Bernard is mentioned in close proximity to a classic statement of Luther's developing Theology of the Cross in the Scholia on Psalm 118 (119):45: 'He crucifies and kills, so that he may revive and glorify. Thus he does a work that is foreign to him so that he may do his own work (*alienum opus eius ab eo, ut faciat opus suum*) (Isa. 28:21). As blessed Bernard correctly said, the divine consolation is delicate and is not given to those who grant access to an alien one. Therefore you must be ... found entirely in the cross and judgments on the old man if you want to walk at large according to the new

---

[50] *WA* 3.175.31–3.
[51] *WA* 3.480.35–481.19.
[52] *WA* 4.74.21–30.
[53] Luther mentions it at *WA* 3.416ff. and 3.420.14–16 during the exposition of Ps. 68 (69).
[54] This idea is found in Augustine as well as Bernard. Bernard thought the end was to come soon, if it had not already broken through. Cf. Bell, *Divus Bernhardus*, p. 46.

man.'[55] When Luther thinks of the dialectic between God's proper and his strange work, his mind turns to Bernard of Clairvaux.[56]

This survey suggests that Luther found many of the themes of his developing Theology of the Cross in his encounter with the monastic spirituality of Bernard of Clairvaux. Luther learnt from him a 'passion piety',[57] dedicated to the growth of humility. The distinctive Bernardian form of this standard late medieval virtue bound it closely to a true self-knowledge, finding its purest form in the crucified Christ, growing out of the experience of humiliation deliberately employed by God for that purpose, and leading to the giving of grace. Because the contemplation on Christ's sufferings leads to the growth of humility, it is the task of the Christian and the church not to scrutinize God or Christ in glory, but in weakness and suffering.

Conclusion

In the development of his theology of the cross, Luther's debt to late medieval monastic and popular Christian life was owed not so much to its theology, but to its spirituality – its patterns of prayer and devotion. Luther's increasingly marked divergence from *theological* aspects of these traditions (whether in passion meditation or in Bernard) shows that division very clearly.

The young Luther's problem can be described as his experience of *dissonance* between this late medieval spiritual tradition and the theology that underpinned it. On several occasions he even describes this sense of being at war within himself.[58] On the one hand, this spirituality, learnt from sources such as later medieval

---

[55]WA 4.331.13–18.

[56]See Erich Kleineidam, 'Ursprung und Gegenstand der Theologie bei Bernhard von Clairvaux und Martin Luther', in Ernst Wilhelm, Feiereis Konrad and Fritz Hoffmann (eds), *Dienst der Vermittlung. Festschrift zum 25-jährigen Bestehen des Philosophisch-Theologischen Studiums im Priesterseminar Erfurt* (Leipzig: St. Benno-Verlag, 1977), pp. 221–47 and Reinhard Schwarz, 'Luther's Inalienable Inheritance of Monastic Theology', *American Benedictine Review* 39 (1988): 430–50.

[57]Franz Posset, 'Monastic Influence on Martin Luther', *Monastic Studies* 18 (1988): 136–63 (139).

[58]E.g. in the Romans commentary, while discussing his former difficulties with scholastic theology: '*non potui intelligere, quomodo me peccatorem similem ceteris deberem reputare et ita nemini me preferre, cum essem contritus et confessus ... Ita mecum pugnavi*'. WA 56.274.2–11.

passion meditation and St Bernard, taught him constantly to examine his sins, to despair of himself so that he would acquire humility, to value suffering as God's way of making him penitent. The
cross represented just this pattern of humbling and humiliation. On
the other hand, his nominalist theology, particularly its soteriology, taught him to value works of contrition, penance, indulgences,
masses, to nurture the growth of humility as a virtue, and to try
to love God above all else 'from his own natural powers', in other
words, doing what he could – doing *quod in se est* – 'what lay
within him', to develop his own internal virtue and merit. Within
the young Luther, therefore, a spirituality of self-accusation lived
uncomfortably alongside a theology of self-justification. What his
spirituality led him to accentuate (his own nothingness and worth-
lessness before God), his theology told him to deny. It was not just
his experience (as has sometimes been suggested),[59] but the spirituality that he had learnt, which was at odds with the prevailing
theological resources available to interpret it. Due to this mismatch,
theological concepts such as the righteousness of God, penitence,
even the cross as an example, which were intended as consolatory,
became terrifying. Luther found in them not peace of heart, but
uncertainty and despair over his ultimate salvation, because they
set before him a standard of holiness that his spirituality taught
him he could never achieve. Luther found himself caught between a
spirituality and a soteriology that he increasingly felt to be mutually
incompatible.

One of these had to go, and it was the soteriology of the *via
moderna* that finally gave way. This spirituality did not remain
unchanged, however. Luther's response to this crisis was a theological reworking of late medieval spirituality, its understanding both
of humility and of the cross. Some elements of this spirituality were
rejected, yet other elements, as we have seen in both passion meditation and in Bernard, helped him to move beyond it. He radicalized
these spiritual traditions, and in the process took them far beyond
both the *via moderna* and even the *via antiqua* of the Thomists,
who had held the line against the synergistic soteriology of much
late medieval theology. This response was, in fact, the development

---

[59]E.g. the extended critique of Luther and the absolutizing of his personality and experience in Joseph Lortz, *Die Reformation in Deutschland*, 6th edn (Freiburg: Herder,
1982), pp. 381–437.

of the Theology of the Cross. The *theologia crucis* can therefore in part be seen as a revolt or protest of popular and monastic piety against the dominant privatized speculative theology of late medieval scholasticism. Luther's Theology of the Cross, which stands so close to the heart of his Reformation discovery is both a break from and continuous with significant elements of popular late medieval religion. Luther is more medieval than we sometimes think, yet he transformed these late medieval traditions into a theology that spoke long to the modern age.

5

Luther on Pilgrimage

Protestants do not go on pilgrimages – at least that's the common perception. In fact, many Protestants do go on pilgrimage, although they rarely call it that. The majority of visitors to the Holy Land, for example, are Protestants from North America, Great Britain or Europe, yet many of them feel uncomfortable with the word 'pilgrimage' to describe what they are doing. Confronted by the language of 'holy places', 'shrines' and the tendency to erect ornate churches on any spot with a claim to Christian antiquity or significance, many Protestants feel disquieted, choosing politely to ignore the ideology of pilgrimage, calling their trip instead a 'study tour' or something equally neutral.

Much of this originates, of course, in the strong critique of pilgrimage mounted by Luther and others within the Protestant Reformation, although it is important to realize that criticism of pilgrimage has its roots further back. Even at the very origins of Christian pilgrimage in the patristic period, Gregory of Nyssa voiced loudly his doubts about the whole exercise,[1] and in the middle ages, figures as diverse as Thomas à Kempis,[2] Jan Hus[3] and Erasmus of Rotterdam[4] all had critical things to say about the

---

[1]Gregory of Nyssa, 'On Pilgrimage', in P. Schaff and H. Wace (eds), *The Life and Writings of Gregory of Nyssa,* Nicene and Post-Nicene Fathers, 2nd Series, vol. 5 (Grand Rapids: Eerdmans, 1892), pp. 382–3.
[2]Thomas À Kempis, *The Imitation of Christ* (Glasgow: Fount, 1977), p. 216 (IV.I).
[3]See Hus's treatise 'On Simony', which he defines as 'trafficking in holy things', with its implied critique of indulgences and pilgrimages to holy sites, in M. Spinka (ed.), *Advocates of Reform: From Wyclif to Erasmus,* Library of Christian Classics, vol. 14 (London: SCM, 1953), pp. 196–278.
[4]Erasmus, 'Enchiridion', in Spinka, *Advocates of Reform,* pp. 337–8, 348.

theological inconsistency and moral sleaze associated with medieval pilgrimage.

Delving into the works of Luther, Calvin or any other of the magisterial reformers, it does not take long to find a very negative estimation of pilgrimage. A typical case is Luther's trenchant opposition to the practice in 'To the Christian Nobility of the German Nation' of 1520:

> All pilgrimages should be dropped. There is no good in them: no commandment enjoins them, no obedience attaches to them. Rather do these pilgrimages give countless occasions to commit sin and to despise God's commandments. This is why there are so many beggars who commit all kinds of mischief by going on these pilgrimages.[5]

Or even more briefly: 'There is no need at all to make a distant pilgrimage or to seek holy places.'[6] Faced with such an apparently total rejection of the practice, subsequent Protestantism has inherited a deep suspicion of the idea, which is hard to shake off, and persuaded many to avoid pilgrimage altogether, as at best unnecessary, at worst downright dangerous. Yet is there more to be said about the Protestant critique of pilgrimage? What, in fact, lay behind the Reformers' objections to the contemporary pilgrimages with which they were familiar? Can pilgrimage be rehabilitated within the structure of Protestant theology? This chapter seeks to examine the basis of the Reformation critique of pilgrimage, a task that has seldom been done in any depth.[7] It asks why the Reformers rejected pilgrimage, and whether their anxieties about late medieval pilgrimage entail a complete and final rejection of pilgrimage. It shows how Luther reimagined this staple practice of medieval spirituality in the light of the gospel of Christ.

---

[5]LW 44.171.
[6]LW 44.40.
[7]An example can be found in J. G. Davies, Pilgrimage Yesterday and Today: Why? Where? How? (London: SCM, 1988), pp. 96–108, which gives a useful overview, but does not delve very deeply into the theological objections to pilgrimage in the Reformation.

Luther on Pilgrimage

While the Reformation spread far and wide beyond the limits that Martin Luther wanted to place on it, the German Reformer remained, as long as he lived, the instigator and inspiration for the rest of the movement. In his early writings, Luther displays a fairly ambivalent approach to pilgrimage, verging on mild approval. In 1518, the year after the storm had broken over his publication of the *95 Theses on the Abuse of Indulgences*, Luther felt he needed to explain his position more fully to guard against misinterpretation. The result was the *Explanations of the 95 Theses*, in which he raises the contemporary practice of pilgrimage to sites such as Santiago de Compostela in Spain, Aachen or Trier in Germany, and Jerusalem in the Holy Land. Luther proceeds to discuss the issue in fairly neutral tones. He outlines a number of false reasons why people go on pilgrimage, including idle curiosity (thoroughly bad), seeking indulgences ('bearable' but not a very good idea) and 'a longing for affliction, and labour for one's sin', which Luther considers a rare, but worthy, reason for going on pilgrimage. Finally, he offers a valid reason for setting out, namely, 'if a man is motivated by a singular devotion for the honour of the saints, the glory of God, and his own edification'.[8] What distinguishes good pilgrimage from bad is motivation. If a pilgrim sets off with the desire to glorify God, or even to edify his own faith, then pilgrimage can be a good and helpful exercise. If he undertakes a pilgrimage in order to gain merit of any kind before God, then it is downright harmful.

Later in the same treatise, Luther goes on to indicate that he does not condemn pilgrimage to sites where relics of Christ and the saints are kept, but at the same time laments the fact these are often done to the exclusion of centring devotion on the best relic that Christ has left behind: the experience of suffering. This is a common theme of Luther's writing at this early stage of his theological development, and reflects the significance of the theology of the cross in his early work. To prepare for God's grace sinners must not try to multiply works of devotion, instead they must allow God to do his work – to humble them through despair, doubt and suffering until they reach the point when they realize their own emptiness before

---

[8]*LW* 31.199.

God and cry out for mercy. Hence, suffering is the most excellent relic of all, the place where we find God's grace.

All this certainly falls short of an enthusiastic recommendation of pilgrimage. However, Luther does not condemn it out of hand. In subsequent years, as his controversy with the papacy gathered pace and significance, however, he began to distance himself sharply from many practices of late medieval piety, and his statements on pilgrimage soon become more polemical and negative. Luther's developing critique consists of four broad objections.

The chief reason why Luther recommends the abolition of pilgrimages is that in his own time, the practice had become inextricably linked with the very theology of merit and 'works', which, as we have already seen, was the opposite of the gospel. One of the chief expressions of that mistaken theology was the doctrine common among the theologians of the *via moderna*, among whom Luther gained his early theological training, that if a sinner does what he can, God will not deny the reward of his grace.[9] In a comment on Genesis 8:22, Luther cites this mistaken belief as the reason why pilgrimages have multiplied:

> From this perverse opinion have originated many dangerous assertions, even some that are clearly false and ungodly, as, for instance, when they maintain: 'When a man does that of which he is capable, God gives grace without fail.' With this trumpet signal, as it were, they have urged men on to prayers, fastings, bodily tortures, pilgrimages, and the like. Thus the world was convinced that if men did as much as they were able to do by nature, they were earning grace, if not by the merit of condignity, then by the merit of congruity.[10]

The main distinguishing mark of Luther's thought over against that of most late medieval theology was his denial that human merit had anything to do with salvation. No late medieval theologian believed in 'justification by works' if that is taken to mean justification by human works alone. All theological systems, whether Thomist, Scotist, Humanist or Nominalist, offered some variation on the

---

[9]The Latin phrase usually ran '*facientibus quod in se est, Deus non denegat gratiam*'.
[10]*LW* 2.123 (Gen. 8:21).

theme that justification was the result of some form of cooperation between God's grace and human endeavour, which transformed individuals and enabled them to progress towards salvation. Luther broke from this altogether, insisting that justification was granted by God not on the basis of human merit, no matter how much it was assisted by God's grace, but instead, on the basis of the merits of Christ – an external, not an internal, righteousness. Pilgrimage had become closely intertwined with the very theological system that Luther opposed, so that to go on pilgrimage had become one of the works that was deemed meritorious or advantageous before God:

> That is the reason for so many monastic orders, cloisters, temples, pilgrimages, and much more. At the bottom of this lies the false notion that these works justify and save. They are steeped in the illusion that such works and the monastic life merit eternal life and redemption from sin and death.[11]

For Luther, such a theology was pastorally and soteriologically disastrous. It led to an anxious uncertainty about salvation, never at rest, never satisfied, whereas the Christian's true birthright was a confident and sure knowledge of God's good will to justify and save through the merits of Christ, despite human sin and failure. For him, the practice of late medieval pilgrimage, whether within his native Germany or wider afield to the great shrines of Christendom, had become almost inextricably entwined with what he felt was a damaging and dangerous theology. Pilgrimages undertaken as part of penance or in fulfilment of a vow were seen, in the popular mind at least, as a meritorious work that would be rewarded with grace, and the desire to acquire such grace had become the dominant motivation for undertaking such journeys. Contemporary pilgrimage had become so infected with 'works righteousness' that it was better to discontinue the practice altogether.

A second reason why Luther rejected pilgrimage was that in focusing on particular geographical locations, it could divert attention from the places where God reveals himself. Luther laments the fact that so many Christians of his day troop off to Compostela or Rome, as if they will find God there, but cannot be found within

---

[11]*LW* 23.171 (Jn. 6:63).

their own local church. On one level, Luther's point here is eschatological. Since the coming of Christ and the Holy Spirit, worship and knowledge of God is no longer confined to one place as they were under the old dispensation. It is therefore unnecessary to visit Jerusalem or any other specific geographical location to find God, as had been necessary in Old Testament times. Luther is eloquent on this point, as he writes of

> the villainy which lured us to Rome, Compostela and Jerusalem, thinking up one pilgrimage after another. This is where the people were to go and pray, just as though we could not find God at home, in our bedroom or wherever we happened to be. God is no longer confined to one place, as He was when He chose to dwell in Jerusalem before the advent of the true temple, Christ the Lord. Thus we read: 'The hour is coming when neither on this mountain nor in Jerusalem will you worship the Father in spirit and in truth' (John 4:21–23). The temple in Jerusalem is no more, and now God must be worshiped wherever one happens to be ... For if Christ is sitting at the right hand of His Father, why, then, should we seek Him in Rome, in Compostela, in Aachen, or at the Oak? You will not find God there; you will find the devil. For God will not let Himself be found in a place of our own choice and choosing.[12]

Luther's point here moves from the eschatological (in the new age, God can now be encountered anywhere) to the sacramental (God has, in fact, told us where to find him). While it is true that God can be found anywhere, his presence is focused in particular places; however, these are not so much geographical but theological locations. For Luther, creation acts like a mask (*larva*), which both conceals and reveals the presence of God. Fallen human reason, however, is liable to misread the signs of God's presence behind creation, so God has designated certain places where he is specifically to be found, and where his will and purpose can be made plain for all to see and understand. These particular sacramental places are identified as the Word, the water of baptism, the bread and wine of the Eucharist, and the people of God. It is to these places that he

---

[12]*LW* 22.250 (Jn. 2:22).

has directed people to go if they are to find him. As Luther points out in 'The Babylonian Captivity of the Church' of 1520, all that is needed for living the Christian life is found in the local church:

> Let every man stay in his own parish; there he will find more than in all the shrines, even if they were all rolled into one. In your own parish you find baptism, the sacrament, preaching and your neighbour, and these things are greater than all the saints in heaven ... Let him stay at home in his own parish church and be content with the best; his baptism, the gospel, his faith, his Christ, and his God, who is the same God everywhere.[13]

As Luther saw it, the medieval pilgrimage industry was both fuelled by and, in turn, fed dissatisfaction with the local church. It fostered a sense of spiritual restlessness and ingratitude, where, not content with the gracious provision God had made for Christians in the normal practice of a local church, the pilgrim was always looking for something else, something extra, beyond what God had provided. More than this though, it was a refusal to look for God in the very places where he had committed himself to be found, and instead insisting that God be found in places of human choosing.

A third critique of pilgrimage centred on the necessary obligations of Christian vocation. Not only had pilgrimages become a distraction from the ways in which God had revealed himself in Word, Sacrament and Church, but they also encouraged escapism from the true duties of the Christian life. Luther often cites the tendency to spend vast amounts of time and money on pilgrimages, which are not commanded in Scripture, and that would have been better spent on helping the poor, one's own family or neighbour, which, of course, is commanded. Luther depicts an ordinary penitent going to confession with his local priest, and finding himself commanded to go on a (relatively expensive) barefoot pilgrimage to Rome as part of his penance for sin. On returning home after confession he sees his neighbour's family in poverty and pain, in dire need of food and finance. Luther's advice is unequivocal: 'He should look to the love of Christ, help him, and let the pilgrimage go.'[14] Commenting on the story of Abraham and Sarah in Genesis 18, Luther contrasts St

---

[13]*LW* 44.187.
[14]*LW* 51.107.

Jerome's pilgrimages to desert places, normally viewed as meritorious and praiseworthy, with Sarah's ordinary hospitality towards guests from her own hearth. For Luther, the latter, much more 'ordinary', task is of much greater value in the eyes of God.[15]

The Reformation was characterized to a large degree by a move away from specifically religious activities towards social ones, and much of this can be traced back to Luther himself. He could even describe the sum of Christian life as 'faith ... directed towards God and love towards man and one's neighbour'.[16] A central aspect of the Reformation critique of late medieval piety concerned its excessive focus on religious works, which took up valuable time, energy and money that would have been better spent on relief for the poor or ordinary acts of generosity and kindness towards one's neighbours or family.[17] For Luther, one of the great benefits of the doctrine of justification by faith alone was that it freed the Christian from the necessity of religious works that needed to be performed in order to aid the process of justification. In this way, Christian energies could be liberated for true acts of service and kindness to others. Works motivated in this way also had greater integrity. They were no longer performed out of a desire for individual salvation, using the neighbour as an instrument to acquire personal piety or merit. Instead they could be performed out of genuine love and compassion for the neighbour, now that the question of justification was settled elsewhere, through faith.

Pilgrimages were one of the many time- and money-consuming activities of late medieval religion that Luther felt had become a serious distraction from acts of true Christian service. They had become a diversion from the real focus of Christian life, in the building up of other people and the Christian community.

A fourth reason Luther decided against pilgrimages concerns the financial corruption that so often clung to pilgrimage sites. As a relatively young friar, Luther had visited Rome on a small business errand, connected with the inner working of his own Augustinian order. On several occasions, he remembered how disappointed he

---

[15]*LW* 3.216.
[16]*LW* 51.75.
[17]See B. A. Gerrish, 'By Faith Alone: Medium and Message in Luther's Gospel', *The Old Protestantism and the New: Essays on the Reformation Heritage* (Edinburgh: T&T Clark, 1982), p. 89.

had been with what he had found there: 'At Rome, men do not find a good example, only pure scandal.'[18] Pilgrimage to the famous centre of the Christian world actually did more harm than good as visitors saw for themselves the decadence and filth of the place. The experience seemed to colour his view of pilgrimage from then on. In his *To the Christian Nobility of the German Nation* of 1520, Luther repeats the charge that one of the main results of pilgrimage is to 'strengthen greed' and to fill the coffers of avaricious bishops.[19] Over time, his views did not soften. In his commentary on John's Gospel in 1537, the same note is sounded. Commenting on the commodification of religion under the papacy, Luther complains: 'This has degenerated into extortion. Special letters of dispensation are issued, brotherhoods and communities are organized, pilgrimages are undertaken, and all sorts of fairs are instituted – all of which nets a great amount of money.'[20]

Again, contemporary pilgrimage had fallen into serious disrepute. It had become associated with some very unsavoury company. And again, because of the seriousness of this charge of severe corruption within medieval pilgrimage, most of which Luther interpreted as a money-making scam by avaricious priests and prelates, and which brought little if any benefit to the participants, he recommended as a result, that wise Christians will desist from going on pilgrimage altogether.

Calvin on Pilgrimage

To help clarify Luther's objections to pilgrimage, it may help to contrast his arguments to those used by John Calvin, who strikes similar notes when he comments on pilgrimage, yet for different reasons. His comments on the practice are not as numerous as Luther's, and seldom does he dwell on the practice long enough to mount a thorough critique of it. Characteristically, 'pilgrimage' occurs in long lists of other aspects of late medieval piety that Calvin wants to turn away from, such as masses for the dead, candles lit in front of shrines or sprinklings of holy water. As a second-generation

---

[18]*LW* 44.170.
[19]*LW* 44.184.
[20]*LW* 22.220 (Jn. 2:14).

reformer, Calvin was less clearly in the forefront of the attack on pilgrimage than Luther, and there is a sense in Calvin's writings of this as a battle that has already been fought, and is no longer a central issue.

Nevertheless, Calvin does have some charges to make against pilgrims and medieval pilgrimage. Like Luther, he comments on the corruption and licentiousness that often accompany pilgrimage,[21] and stresses that pilgrimage is nowhere commanded in Scripture.[22] He goes beyond this, and even beyond Luther, in suggesting that a scriptural text such as John 4:21 actually prohibits pilgrimage, though it is significant that the target of his attack in this and on many other occasions is specifically *votive* pilgrimages, which were undertaken as a result of a vow.[23] Another aspect of contemporary pilgrimage that Calvin dislikes is the idea that a pilgrimage remains meritorious or valid, regardless of the state of the heart:

> And thus, if a monk rise from the bed of his adultery to chant a few psalms without one spark of godliness in his breast, or if a whore-monger, a thief, or any foresworn villain, seeks to make reparation for his crimes by mass or pilgrimage, they would be loath to consider this lost labour. By God, on the other hand, such a disjunction of the form from the inward sentiment of devotion is branded as sacrilege.[24]

A particular aspect of pilgrimage considered at some length by Calvin is the widespread medieval interest in relics of the saints and apostles in his *Treatise on Relics* of 1543. Implicit within this critique is an attack on pilgrimage to holy sites possessing such collections of relics, which was an integral part of the whole industry. This piece is a remarkable catalogue of the location of various collections of relics across Europe, not, of course, as a guidebook for

---

[21]John Calvin, *Calvin's Commentaries on the Twelve Minor Prophets*, trans. J. Owen (Edinburgh: Calvin Translation Society, 1847), Hos. 4.14.
[22]See, e.g. John Calvin, *Calvin's Commentaries on the Book of Psalms*, trans. J. Anderson (Edinburgh: Calvin Translation Society, 1844), Acts 14:3, p. 3, and Calvin, *Calvin's Commentaries on the Twelve Minor Prophets*, Jon. 1:16, pp. 69–70.
[23]Cf., e.g. John Calvin, *The Institutes of the Christian Religion*, John T. McNeill (ed.), Library of Christian Classics; 2 vols, trans. Ford Lewis Battles (Westminster John Knox, 1960), 1.11.10.
[24]Calvin, *Calvin's Commentaries on the Book of Psalms*, Ps. 50:16, p. 275.

those who would wish to visit, but as a piece of subversive detective work to destroy such interest. Calvin takes great delight in pointing out how an arm of St Anthony, formerly kissed and venerated in Geneva, turned out to be the bone of a stag; how there are at least fourteen nails from the cross being exhibited in different places, and how most of the apostles must have had two or three bodies to provide the scattered catalogue of bones and skulls on show in the various pilgrimage centres of Europe. The treatise is designed to uncover the unscrupulousness of those who put forward such fakes for veneration, and the credulity of those who visit them. More important, however, are Calvin's cautionary remarks about the relic trade, which have a primarily theological rather than an ethical focus.

> But the first abuse, and, as it were, beginning of the evil, was, that when Christ ought to have been sought in his Word, sacraments, and spiritual influences, the world, after its wont, clung to his garments, vests and swaddling clothes; and thus overlooking the principal matter, followed only its accessory.[25]

His point is similar to that of Luther's mentioned above, that pilgrimage to sites where relics of Christ and the saints are on display has an inbuilt tendency to deflect attention away from the places where God has chosen to make himself known and available to us – most notably in the word and sacraments – and on to lesser things. His fear is that a preoccupation with trivia will lead to the worship of trivia, rather than adoration of the true God. Calvin is fully aware of the positive motivation that lies behind much devotion to relics, namely, the desire to keep alive the memory of and devotion to Christ and the saints. However, 'the desire for relics', he concludes, 'is usually the parent of idolatry'. An intense focus on these items will almost inevitably, he thinks, lead to a fascination for them. Such fascination inevitably draws attention and devotion to the relics themselves (which, in most cases, are bogus anyway), and away from a devotion to Christ, who alone is worthy of worship. To call such objects 'sacramental' and to validate devotion to them in this way is, for Calvin, to miss the point. True sacraments

---

[25]John Calvin, 'Treatise on Relics', *Tracts and Treatises on the Reformation of the Church* (Edinburgh: Oliver & Boyd, 1844), p. 289.

are those places where God has directed us to find him. For Calvin, the water of baptism and the bread and wine of the Lord's Supper enjoy a special status as means of grace, as spaces where the unity between Christ and the believer is both demonstrated and enacted, precisely because they enjoy divine institution. We are not at liberty to create our own sacraments: 'All divine worship of man's devising, having no better and surer foundation than his own opinion, be its semblance of wisdom what it may, is mere vanity and folly.'[26] For Calvin, this is a cardinal theological principle – it safeguards the freedom and initiative of God, and is an expression of the fundamental futility of human attempts to establish means of approaching God on our own terms.

It is perhaps characteristic of Calvin's theology that it is he rather than Luther who mounts a sustained attack on pilgrimage to collections of relics. Calvin's theology always had a tendency to assert the spiritual nature of worship of God, whereas Luther was more cautious about dividing physical from spiritual reality, so much so that he could write that 'the Spirit cannot be with us except in material and physical things such as the Word, water and Christ's body and in his saints on earth.'[27] In addition, Luther always had to be a little careful about relics, as his chief patron in the early years, Frederick the Wise, possessed a very large collection of them, kept in the Castle Church at the other end of the main street in Wittenberg from Luther's Augustinian friary. However, Luther's and Calvin's positions are not very far apart and they combine to sound a rigorous and robust note of caution about the practice of pilgrimage that has had a huge influence on the history of pilgrimage since the sixteenth century, and remains influential on the many Protestants who visit pilgrimage sites today but do not feel entirely at ease doing so.

The Reformation and Pilgrimage Today

This survey of the thought of the two major figures within the Protestant Reformation of the sixteenth century presents a common

---

[26]Calvin, 'Treatise on Relics', p. 290.
[27]*LW* 37.95.

front, but for different reasons. As we might expect, given the different cast of their theologies, Luther and Calvin focus on different aspects of pilgrimage as they mount their critique. Luther condemns the exercise primarily because it has become tied up with a theology of merit, an attempt to justify oneself by religious works, thus compromising the central article of justification by faith alone. For Calvin, on the other hand, given the centrality in his theology of the proper worship of Christ, as the place in which God makes his benefits available to us, it is the tendency of pilgrimage to attract worship to irrelevant accessories rather than the main thing itself, which is it Achilles's heel. It might be said that for Luther the chief sin was unbelief, whereas for Calvin it was idolatry. These theological perspectives are reflected clearly in their respective (and complementary) objections to pilgrimage.

Of the two, Calvin's is the more fundamental objection. His critique rests on a more basic problem – that focusing on a particular object or place has the potential of distracting attention from Christ himself. As we have seen, in other (sacramental) contexts, Luther stressed quite emphatically the capacity of physical things to convey the real presence of God, and so, in principle, he has fewer difficulties with the idea of particular places or objects as being helpful or beneficial to faith. Similarly, Calvin tends in general to take a stricter line on Scriptural permission – what is not in Scripture tends to be frowned on – whereas Luther could often permit practices not explicitly outlawed by the Bible.

Although different in focus, there is a large degree of overlap in the two theologians' evaluation of pilgrimage. Put together, their arguments also sound fairly conclusively like a comprehensive denial of the value of the practice altogether. Yet on closer inspection, the attack on pilgrimage found in these Reformation thinkers is more strictly speaking an attack on the abuse of pilgrimage, rather than on pilgrimage itself. Luther's arguments focus on the close connection between contemporary pilgrimage and a theology of justification by meritorious works. His additional arguments, that pilgrimages distract attention from the designated place of God's revealed presence, from works of true Christian love and piety and his protest at the financial corruption entailed, all have a similar character. In other words, Luther's critique does not argue that pilgrimage in itself is fundamentally wrong, just that it has become so entangled with damaging and dangerous habits of thought and life that it would be better to desist altogether. In fact, Luther says as much in his treatise *To the Christian Nobility* of 1520: 'I say this not because pilgrimages are bad, but because they are ill-advised at this time.'[28] In context, this statement refers to pilgrimage to Rome, and Luther adds an instruction that 'no-one should be allowed to make such a pilgrimage for reasons of curiosity or his own pious devotion, unless it is first acknowledged by his parish priest, his town authorities, or his overlord that he has a good and sufficient reason for doing so.'[29] There is no evidence that such an arrangement was ever formally instituted, yet the point is that Luther acknowledges here the possibility of 'good and sufficient reason' for going on pilgrimage. Luther is clearly concerned to prevent the damage caused by embarking on pious journeys for the wrong reasons, yet he leaves open the possibility of doing so for the right reasons. Unlike Indulgences, where Luther's initial attack was on their abuse, but which he later condemned altogether, Luther never goes this second step with pilgrimage. For him, it remained a practice damned by association.

As we have seen, Calvin comes closer than Luther to a total ban on pilgrimage. However, the main lines of his case can also be understood as primarily aimed at the abuse rather than at the practice itself. In his robust critique of the relic trade, he attacks not so much pilgrimage in itself, as pilgrimage to pious souvenirs, which are often bogus, and a severe distraction from true faith and piety. The fact that many of his cited references to pilgrimage are to 'votive pilgrimage' indicates that one of his principle objections is to the element of compulsion involved. For him, as for Luther, pilgrimage is nowhere commanded in Scripture, and Calvin sees the performance for vows to undertake such journeys as an infringement of the liberty of a Christian and a mistaken attempt to earn merit or fulfil legal requirements that had no place in a theology of faith. Again, Calvin too is eloquent on the sexual and financial abuse that sometimes accompanied pilgrimage, and was a strong critic of pilgrimage undertaken where the heart was not engaged along with the body and the feet. Pilgrimage that detracts from spiritual attention to and worship of Christ is, in Calvin's mind, to be

---

[28]*LW* 44.169–70.
[29]*LW* 44.169.

resisted. However, again, this leaves open the question of whether a form of pilgrimage can be found that avoids such a tendency.

It might be useful to think of the Reformation critique of medieval pilgrimage by imagining a delicate flowering plant that has become tightly entangled with some aggressive and dangerous weeds. The weeds are so dangerous, and so inextricably tangled up with the plant, that the only remedy is to pull up plant and weeds together. Better to have nothing at all than a pleasant flower that has merely become a climber for poisonous weeds, especially as the plant is not essential to the garden in the first place. The question remains, however, of whether, with some distance of time, when conditions are very different, the plant can be re-rooted in good soil that can be kept clear of the weeds that damaged it so much in the past?

Reforming Pilgrimage?

If it is true that the main focus of Luther's and even Calvin's attack on medieval pilgrimage was strictly speaking on abuses rather than the journey itself, another series of questions presents itself. In the light of their critique of the practice, what might a responsible Reformation approach to pilgrimage look like? What might Reformation theology have to say to the contemporary understanding and conduct of pilgrimage today?

It hopefully goes without saying that any introduction to pilgrimage or teaching on the subject needs to carefully avoid any suggestion that the exercise earns any particular merit towards salvation, or indeed affects the constancy of God's compassion or faithfulness in any way. Whereas the *hajj* in Islam enjoys the status of one of the five pillars of that faith, pilgrimage can never become in any sense compulsory for Christians, either by declaration or by implication. Despite the close association between pilgrimage and a theology of merit in the late Middle Ages, it is perfectly possible to engage in pilgrimage without any sense that this carries any kind of special favour with God, or places the pilgrim on any special new spiritual place not enjoyed by those who stay at home. More positively, however, four further points might be made.

The first concerns ethical responsibility. Luther and Calvin, not to mention the countless other less well-known reforming figures of the sixteenth century, drew attention to the corruption that had seeped into the pilgrimage industry. It is perhaps a tendency that always lies close at hand when sensitive and personal subjects such as faith and devotion are present. It is very easy to prey on religious desire and affection, and the space between open-hearted faith and simple credulity is one that many unscrupulous traders looking for a quick profit are happy to fill. In the last century, on his visit to the Holy Land, Mark Twain complained of how the pilgrim's 'life is almost badgered out of him by importunate swarms of beggars and pedlars, who hang in the strings to one's sleeves and coat-tails, and shriek and shout in his ears'.[30] It is a description that will sound very familiar to any contemporary pilgrim who has visited the main sites in the Holy Land or many other traditional pilgrimage destinations at the height of the tourist season. Pilgrimage has attracted its fair share of unscrupulous trade, and, at times, pilgrimage guides have often been tempted to stretch credulity by claiming more than is warranted for particular sites or objects. Open-minded and open-hearted faith is necessarily vulnerable to abuse. If it becomes cynical and jaundiced from the outset, it loses something essential to its own character. The Reformation critique of the ethics of pilgrimage comes as a healthy and necessary reminder of the openness of faith to exploitation, its susceptibility to being taken for a ride, and the need for simplicity and honesty on the part of both host and visitor to enable the experience to be as beneficial as possible.

A second issue centres on Luther's concern that pilgrimage encouraged dissatisfaction with the local church, and his insistence that it should not replace acts of kindness and generosity to one's neighbour, friend or fellow Christian. This serves as a reminder that pilgrimage needs to take with the utmost seriousness the Christian communities both *from* which the pilgrim leaves and *to* which he or she visits. It is sadly common for Western visitors to the Holy Land to visit all the main biblical sites, but never to exchange a word with a local Christian, Arab or Jew. Visitors can equally be rushed in and out of pilgrimage sites with no thought for the impact that their visit has on the local area or the need to support the local Christian

---

[30]Mark Twain, *The Innocents Abroad, or the New Pilgrim's Progress* (Hartford, CT: American, 1869), p. 602.

community, whether economically or in prayer. Luther's insistence on the necessity that pilgrimage contributes to, rather than detracts from, local Christian communities might serve as a reminder to Christian tour companies to design itineraries that deliberately enable supportive contact with local Christians. Similarly, pilgrimage must not detract from or foster dissatisfaction with home churches.

There is a paradox to be found at the heart of pilgrimage. A pilgrim goes in search of a closer knowledge, experience or relationship with God. However, a common outcome of good, healthy pilgrimage is a renewed and strengthened sense that God can, in fact, be found not just in so-called holy places, but anywhere. Since the coming of the Spirit, God can now be found wherever his people meet. The temple where he is pleased to dwell can be found wherever the body of Christ now meets (1 Cor. 3:16, 6:19). Responsible tour leaders will bear this in mind constantly, crafting the expectations and outcomes of a tour plan to strengthen rather than weaken attachment, commitment and practical action within and from local churches back home.

Third, Calvin's cautionary remarks about relics and Christian gullibility may strike us as unnecessarily scathing. The relic industry is nothing like as widespread today, and a certain healthy scepticism is fairly common about some of the more outlandish claims made for pilgrimage sites or artefacts. Nevertheless, it is hard to deny that it remains distinctly possible to encourage an unhealthy, voyeuristic fascination with places and objects in modern-day pilgrim tours. Many a Christian visitor to the Holy Land has found themselves wondering whether or not this really was the cave where Jesus was born, the mountain where he fed the five thousand or the route he took through Jerusalem carrying his cross. It is possible to spend one's entire time in the Church of the Holy Sepulchre worried about questions of architectural and archaeological authenticity and miss completely the opportunity to reflect on the nature and meaning of the cross and resurrection of Christ in the place where Christians have come for centuries to recall and experience in some extended way, those very epochal events. Fascination with precise locations can do precisely what Calvin was afraid of – lead subtly away from the worship of Christ, to attention to trivia, which, however interesting, fails to promote holiness or transformation.

One of the effects of good pilgrimage to the Holy Land, for example, is a renewed sense of the true humanity of Christ. Some popular

Christianity can verge uncomfortably on the fringes of Docetism. In other words, Jesus is worshipped and sung to as a spiritual, almost imaginary, being who bears little relationship to real life, or to the historical figure who lived in the middle of the complex ferment of first-century Palestine. Visiting the land of Jesus brings home to many a Christian traveller the emphatic earthiness of the real Jesus – that here was a figure deeply engaged with the political, religious and economic issues of his own time, and who died on a real cross in a real city in real history. In other words, responsible pilgrimage can strengthen faith in the reality of the incarnation, in the depth of divine involvement in and commitment to the world in Christ. In this way, far from distracting from Christ in the way which Calvin feared, good, theologically informed pilgrimage can, in fact, refocus attention on and strengthen faith in him.

The fourth point retains the place of pilgrimage as a metaphor for Christian life. By far the majority of Calvin's references to *peregrinatio* do not, in fact, refer to medieval journeys to holy places, but to the Christian life, lived in anticipation of arrival at the heavenly city, from cradle to grave.[31] Pilgrimage as a metaphor for the Christian life has a very long pedigree, and in restoring this as its primary usage, Calvin was only returning to an ancient and respected Christian usage. The Protestant tradition beyond Luther and Calvin explored this metaphor often in great detail, most notably, of course, in John Bunyan's *Pilgrim's Progress* of 1678.

The idea of specifically *Christian* life is that pilgrimage gives it shape and direction, and orients it decisively towards its future rather than its present, the destination rather than travelling for its own sake. It is perhaps a metaphor that needs to be rediscovered in an age that has lost a sense of purpose or direction to any kind of heavenly, or even earthly, city. A church living in a culture that does not see any direction in the future, but instead celebrates the aimlessness of wandering needs good Christian imagery that reminds it again and again of its true calling to live in anticipation and hope, not complacency and contentment.

In these small ways, pilgrims can reappropriate the important role that the notion of pilgrimage has played, not least in the Reformation, as a metaphor for Christian life. Calvin's disdain for

---

[31]For the New Testament roots of this imagery, see e.g. Gal. 4:26, Heb. 11:10, Rev. 21:2.

pilgrimage, which fails to change the heart and the behaviour of participants, reminds us of the need for pilgrimage today not to become like a holiday that is designed to enable us to forget and to escape from the realities awaiting us at home, but, instead, to become an experience that enables the pilgrim to reassess their 'regular' Christian existence, and reorient it to its true identity and goal. It can restore a sense of proper Christian ambition that is dissatisfied with the status quo, and instead determines to anticipate and hope towards the day when the earth will be renewed and the kingdom of God will come in all its fullness.

Luther's and the more general Reformation critique of pilgrimage still needs to be heard today. It still stands as a caution against some of the theological and spiritual pitfalls into which the exercise can fall in the twenty-first as well as in the sixteenth century. Yet at the same time, as we have seen, the critique falls short of a total prohibition of the practice, and in an age where the theological battles have moved onto other grounds, there is scope for the reimagining of pilgrimage as ethically responsible, supportive of local Christian communities, renewing faith in and understanding of Christ and rooted in Christian life as pilgrimage towards the goal of a new heaven and a new earth. Luther's gospel can help us avoid the dangers of pilgrimage yet point us to a new way of imagining it as a practice that does not undermine but truly builds faith.

6

Luther on Prayer

Peter Beskendorf, Luther's barber in Wittenberg, was one of Luther's best friends. Assuming that the rituals of men getting their hair cut have not changed much in 500 years, presumably many conversations rambled on between them as Luther's thick mane of black hair was being shorn. Beskendorf was a serious Christian, not particularly well educated, but eager to learn, and reasonably devout. In 1535, after a conversation in which his friend asked for advice on his prayer life, Luther wrote a short piece titled 'A Simple Way to Pray', written for Beskendorf, and for many others like him. It offers us a fascinating glimpse into Luther's own pattern of prayer, his advice to others learning to establish a life of devotion and how his understanding of the gospel helped reimagine the place of prayer in the life of the Christian.[1]

Luther advises a regular pattern of personal prayer, first thing in the morning and last thing at night, but including prayers at other times as well. He urged his friend to guard against the temptation to delay prayer, the lure of the voice of procrastination. If you listen to that voice, says Luther, 'nothing will come of prayer for that day.'[2] At other times, he particularly sought to pray when he was

---

[1]Compared to other topics, there is a surprisingly small volume of literature on Luther's approach to prayer. Examples include Martin E. Lehmann, *Luther and Prayer* (Milwaukee: Northwestern, 1985); M. J. Haemig, 'Practical Advice on Prayer from Martin Luther', *Word & World* 35:1 (2015): 22–30; M. Rogers, '"Deliver Us from the Evil One": Martin Luther on Prayer', *Themelios* 34:3 (2009): 335–47; and D. M. S. Carr, 'Consideration of the Meaning of Prayer in the Life of Martin Luther', *Concordia Theological Monthly* 42:9 (1971): 620–9.
[2]A Table Talk records him as saying: 'Whenever I happen to be prevented by the press of duties from observing my hour of prayer, the entire day is bad for me.' LW 54.17.

distracted by other things: 'When I feel that I have become cool and
joyless in prayer because of other tasks or thoughts (for the flesh
and the devil always impede and obstruct prayer), I take my little
psalter, hurry to my room, or, if it be the day and hour for it, to the
church where a congregation is assembled and, as time permits,
I say quietly to myself and word-for-word the Ten Commandments,
the Creed, and, if I have time, some words of Christ or of Paul, or
some psalms, just as a child might do.'[3]

Luther often mentioned that his prayer centred around these key
texts of Christian belief and devotion: the recitation of the Lord's
Prayer, the Ten Commandments and the Creed, using each of these
as pegs on which to hang his personal prayer. In 'A Personal Prayer
Book', written in 1522, he wrote about how these worked as a kind
of guidebook to the Christian life. The Commandments served as
the Law, revealing and reminding the Christian how much she has
sinned and needs help; the Creed indicated where help, in other
words grace, could be found; the Lord's Prayer acted as a reassurance that God will provide for every need the Christian encounters
as she lives the Christian life: 'In these three are the essentials of the
Bible.'[4]

The backbone of prayer for Luther was the Lord's Prayer, which
he used most days, with the Creed and Commandments visited
more sparingly. While using these set forms as a structure, he always
varied his prayers, blending liturgical form with his own extempore
requests: 'I say my prayers in one fashion today, in another tomor-
row, depending on my mood and feeling. I stay however, as nearly
as I can, with the same general thoughts and ideas.'[5]

So, for example, he counsels his friend to pray his way through
the Lord's Prayer, using each phrase as a springboard for his own
personal prayers:

Then repeat one part or as much as you wish, perhaps the first
petition: 'Hallowed be thy name,' and say: 'Yes, Lord God, dear
Father, hallowed be thy name, both in us and throughout the
whole world. Destroy and root out the abominations, idolatry,
and heresy of the Turk, the pope, and all false teachers and

---

[3]*LW* 43.193.
[4]*LW* 43.14.
[5]*LW* 43.198.

fanatics who wrongly use thy name and in scandalous ways take it in vain and horribly blaspheme it.'[6]

This writing was one of a series during Luther's career where he wrote in a pastoral, exhortatory mode to urge a reformation of personal prayer. The kind of prayer he advocated was a blend of liturgical form and personal language from the heart. It was determined not just by the words in a prayer book, but also by a person's own mood and temper. It meant prayer that was mentally engaged, not mindless and formal, so that a person praying needed to engage the mind, rather than pray by rote or in some automatic way: 'It is now clear to me that a person who forgets what he has said has not prayed well.'[7] Luther's preferred style of prayer blended aspects of established and traditional forms of prayer, yet placing his own personal stamp on them at the same time. And this was true not just of his own personal prayer, but also the way he thought about prayer for all Christians. As so often when it came to church reform, Luther's practice was not a wholesale abandonment of previous forms of prayer and spirituality, but an adaptation of them in the light of his theological insights into the role of faith, hope and love in the Christian life. Luther's writing on prayer served as a rewriting of traditions of personal prayer with a long history in the medieval past, to deepen its Christian identity. As David Steinmetz put it: 'Before Christendom could become truly Christian, it had to abandon old habits of thinking and acting and embrace a new vision of what being an authentic Christian implied.'[8]

Luther and Medieval Forms of Prayer

Late medieval piety cannot be understood apart from the increasing pace of social, economic, ecclesiastical and spiritual crisis in Europe from the fourteenth century onwards. This, of course, resulted not only in the challenge to the papacy of conciliarism, but also in a range of movements impatient with the complex speculative

---

[6]*LW* 43.195.
[7]*LW* 43.199.
[8]David C. Steinmetz, *Luther in Context*, 2nd edn (Grand Rapids: Baker Academic, 2002), p. 127.

theology of the thirteenth and earlier centuries. These movements, whether the *devotio moderna*, strands of mysticism such as those represented by Meister Eckhardt, Johannes Tauler or Jean Gerson, or even in the spiritual writings of nominalists such as Gabriel Biel, often stemmed from a widespread and frequently Franciscan-inspired desire for the simplicity of an experience-centred Christian devotion as opposed to the seemingly fruitless disputes and confusion of authority in the Church of the Great Schism and Thomist theology. Bonaventure, for example, saw prayer as a way of spiritual ascent: 'By praying in this way, we receive light to discern the steps of the ascent into God.'[9]

These mystical forms of prayer drew Luther's eye, especially when preoccupied with the themes of the Theology of the Cross, as he was in his early years as a theologian, even publishing a version of the distinctly mystical *Theologia Deutsch* in 1516 and 1518. Earlier scholars saw Luther as an enthusiastic advocate of German mysticism, although more recent studies have emphasized how the motivation behind the publication of the *Theologia Deutsch* was as much political as it was spiritual, stemming from a desire that the developing Wittenberg theology could be seen to have roots in genuinely *German* piety, and was therefore continuous with a long and respectable German tradition.

It is more commonly thought today that while Luther used mystical terminology, he filled that language with his own meaning. A number of years ago, Heiko Oberman summed up the argument: 'Reformation scholarship has reached no consensus concerning whether or not Luther ought to be called a mystic.'[10] It seems that Luther was drawn to German mysticism as a forgotten but rich backwater of medieval thought. While he did use German mysticism for political ends, he nonetheless found congenial ideas in these mystics, a theology that stressed experience, the need for self-abandonment before God's will, the initiative of God, passive suffering and the hiddenness of God. There was a seriousness about this form of prayer that attracted him, and at times, his writing on prayer sounds quite similar to such forms.

[9]Bonaventure, *The Soul's Journey into God* (Mahwah, NJ: Paulist Press, 1978), p. 60.
[10]Heiko A. Oberman, *The Reformation: Roots and Ramifications*, trans. Andrew Colin Gow (Edinburgh: T&T Clark, 1994), p. 88.

For example, the prayer he commands to Peter Beskendorf is affective, encouraging a deep sense of attentiveness to God. Prayer needs attention: it is not an easy thing that comes naturally. A Christian needs to prepare his heart and mind for prayer, because it is hard work. If he does not learn to pay attention in prayer, it can be dangerous, just as, as he reminded his reader, if a barber were to lose concentration while shaving a beard, he might just as easily cut the nose or throat of his customer rather than his facial hair. In a saying recorded in the Table Talk, he was struck by his dog Tölpel's ability to fix his eyes rigidly on a piece of meat dangling before his eyes: 'Oh, if I could only pray the way this dog watches the meat! All his thoughts are concentrated on the piece of meat. Otherwise he has no thought, wish, or hope.'[11]

Luther caricatures the kind of distraction that he often experienced in his days as an Augustinian Friar: 'Like the priest who prayed, "*Deus in adjutorium meum intende.* Farmhand, did you unhitch the horses? *Domine ad adjuvandum me festina.* Maid, go out and milk the cow. *Gloria patri et filio et spiritui sancto.* Hurry up, boy, I wish the ague would take you!" I have heard many such prayers in my experience under the papacy; most of their prayers are of this sort. This is blasphemy and it would be better if they played at it if they cannot or do not care to do better.'[12]

Luther's teaching on prayer therefore emphasizes deep attentiveness before God, placing oneself before God in active awareness. His simplest definition of prayer was this: 'Prayer is nothing else than the lifting up of heart or mind to God', or as he put it in the Personal Prayer Book, 'a turning to God frequently and with heartfelt longing, and doing so without ceasing'.[13] Or, as he puts it elsewhere: 'Moreover true prayer happens when the heart, and not just the mind speaks: "spiritual and sincere prayer reflects the heart's innermost desires, its sighing and yearning."'[14]

This is the kind of affective language that could be found in many of the mystics, from the *Imitation of Christ* to Johannes Tauler.

However, there is a difference. Luther has little sense as, for example, Tauler does, that in prayer the soul is lost in God. For

[11] *LW* 54.38.
[12] *LW* 43.198.
[13] *LW* 43.12.
[14] *LW* 42.20.

Tauler, the human spirit 'loses itself so completely that no trace of
the self remains'.[15] In Luther's mind, union with Christ is the result,
not of hours of attentive prayer, but of faith, and he is always nervous of any idea of spiritual ascent through spiritual activity, however pious or well-intentioned. For Luther, the distinction between
God the Creator and us the creature is only overcome in the incarnate Christ and through faith in him, rather than through the use of
any spiritual exercise. For Luther, mystical language always had a
strictly Christological, rather than theological, meaning. It referred
not to the being of God, hidden in mystery, but to the hidden form
of his revelation in Christ.

Despite these differences, there were affinities between Luther
and mystical forms of prayer. A spirituality that was affective rather
than purely cerebral and objective attracted him. Denis Janz has
shown how Luther's critique of Thomas Aquinas centred around
Luther's disdain for a type of theology that seemed insufficiently
emotionally engaged.[16] Luther often contrasted the *affectus* with the
intellectus, favouring an inner emotional engagement with Christ
over a dry objective intellectual detachment.[17] Luther's approach to
prayer had significant overlaps with forms of mystical prayer common in late medieval spirituality.

Luther's Critique of Habits of Prayer

In other ways, Luther sought to wean his readers off other ways of
praying that were common in the piety of the period.

Luther tried every way he could to wean his readers off the idea
that prayer was in any way meritorious. Instead, it was a spiritual exercise that reassured a person of grace, understood as divine
favour. The idea that prayers said, regardless of the state of the
heart, were meritorious is therefore inadmissible: 'If the lifting up of

---

[15]Johannes Tauler, *Sermons* (New Jersey: Paulist Press, 1985), sermon 21, p. 77.
[16]Denis R. Janz, *Luther on Thomas Aquinas: The Angelic Doctor in the Thought of
the Reformer* (Wiesbaden: Franz Steiner, 1989).
[17]e.g. in two Good Friday sermons in 1518: '*Scriptura quoque nos hortatur magis ad
affectum passionis Christi quam intellectum.*' WA 1.343.28–9. '*Ideoque intellectus
non potest capere nec lingua dicere nec littera scribere, sed tantum affectus percipere,
quid sit Christum passum esse: omina enim absorbet infinitum.*' WA 1.344.9–11.

the heart constitutes the essence and nature of prayer, it follows that everything else which does not invite the lifting of the heart is not prayer. Therefore, singing, talking, and whistling, when devoid of the sincere uplifting of the heart, are as unlike prayer as scarecrows in the garden are unlike human beings. The essence is wanting; only the appearance and name are present.'[18]

Luther warns Herr Beskendorf against any kind of prayer that suggests earning any kind of reward, even including direct mystical union with God. 'I urge everyone to break away from using the Bridget prayers and any others which are ornamented with indulgences or rewards and urge all to get accustomed to praying this plain, ordinary Christian prayer. The longer one devotes himself to this kind of praying, the more pleasant and dear it becomes.'[19]

His approach is not a wholesale abandonment of earlier forms of prayer, but their thorough reformation. The *Ave Maria*, for example, part of the staple diet of medieval prayer, can be used as a meditation on the grace that God has given Mary as the mother of God, a means of offering the proper respect for her as the one whose obedience enabled the incarnate Christ to enter the world. However, it is not to be used as a prayer to the Virgin herself, or in any way encouraging any trust in her merits – that is reserved for Christ alone. 'Let not our hearts cleave to her, but through her, penetrate to Christ and to God himself.'[20]

Luther of course rewrote liturgical forms to help churches that wanted to be reformed to worship in appropriate ways, but he also did the same in personal prayer, performing something of a revolution in prayer that affected millions of subsequent Protestants in the following centuries.

So, for example, the 'Personal Prayer Book' was written as a conscious alternative to the myriad books of a similar kind that advocated prayers to saints, the counting up of sins in contrition in preparation for confession, prayers for pilgrimages, indulgences and the like. These books, often handsomely bound, would offer lists of sins to be confessed, prayers to the Virgin Mary, prayers to various saints and martyrs, and accounts of how to acquire merit and gain

---

[18]*LW* 42.25.
[19]*LW* 43.12–13.
[20]*LW* 43.39.

forgiveness. Luther knew these well, and rather than protest against them, decided to try to replace them with him own version:

> These books are puffed up with promises of indulgences and come out with decorations in red ink and pretty titles; one is called *Hortulus animae*, another *Paradisus animae*, and so on. These books need a basic and thorough reformation if not total extermination. And I would make the same judgment about those passionals or books of legends into which the devil has tossed his own additions. But I just don't have the time to undertake such a reformation; it is too much for me alone. So until God gives me more time and grace, I will limit myself to the exhortation in this book.[21]

In 1528, Luther wrote a set of instructions for official visitors to parishes that had adopted the new reforming ways. These visitations were to include an urgent exhortation to the people to pray, and were to involve detailed teaching on the nature of prayer and how it is to be done. We pray, he reminds his readers, primarily because God has commanded us to, but also because God has promised to hear us. Not put off by a sense of one's own unworthiness, the Christian is to pray boldly for both temporal and spiritual things. This faithful, importunate prayer, addressed directly to our heavenly Father who is eager to listen, is contrasted to forms of prayer that do not engage the heart or mind: 'It cannot be called prayer when one repeats heedlessly a great number of *Pater Nosters* or psalms, pays little regard to or places no reliance on God's promise to hear, or does not wait for God's help. Indeed such a one has no God, and it happens to him what Ps. 114 says, "Their idols have ears but do not hear," that is, such a one imagines a god who does not hear.'[22]

While the Lord's Prayer and other forms could be translated into the new spirituality, others could not. Luther clearly honoured Mary as the mother of God, but refused to believe that she played any role in interceding for us, much less being any kind of co-redemptrix. As a result prayers such as the *Ave Maria* were not to be said by good Lutherans, neither were prayers to Mary during

[21]*LW* 43.11–12.
[22]*LW* 40.279.

childbirth. He insists that the Hail Mary should not be used as a prayer or invocation, because they are addressed to Mary rather than to Christ or the Father: 'No one speaks evil of this Mother and her Fruit as much as those who bless her with many rosaries and constantly mouth the Hail Mary. These, more than any others, speak evil against Christ's word and faith in the worst way.'[23] However, it can be used as a meditation, helping us remember what God gave to Mary, and Luther also adds 'a wish that everyone may know and respect her, as one blessed by God'.

Luther warned against the sole use of 'mental prayer' for beginners, extempore prayer issued purely out of the heart and mind, as he knows that distraction soon sets in: 'No one should depend on his heart and presume to pray without uttering words unless he is well trained in the Spirit and has experience in warding off stray thoughts.'[24] Set forms of prayer are useful for those inexperienced in prayer. They are like the wings of a bird that help you soar, until you grow your own feathers and learn to fly yourself. Yet they are not to be mumbled thoughtlessly, as it is vital to engage the heart and mind in prayer, avoiding any sense of pride in one's own piety and spiritual devotion.[25]

How to Pray

In 1519, fairly early in his theological development, Luther wrote a short exposition of the Lord's Prayer, again for the benefit of simple Christians, an 'Exposition of the Lord's Prayer for Simple Laymen'. He prefers prayers that are brief, not lengthy. Long prayers carry the subtle danger that we hope that God will answer because of the length and strength of the prayer, rather than because of his own mercy and grace: 'The fewer the words, the better the prayer. Few words and richness of meaning is Christian; many words and lack of meaning is pagan.'

The beginning of the Lord's Prayer is significant, in that it addresses God with the proper title. We are not taught to address him with the title of Lord, God or Judge, but with Father. This form

---

[23]*LW* 43.40.
[24]*LW* 42.25.
[25]*LW* 42.25–6.

of address places the Christian in the right attitude with regard to God, as a child coming to the father asking for his help and mercy. The child expects the parent to hear, and so included within this form of address is the faith that is expectant for the father's response. 'He who prays thus stands with an upright heart in the correct relationship to God; such a man is able to pray and to move God to mercy.'[26]

Luther contrasts the simplicity of this form of address with the person who rustles through a prayer book, or counting rosary beads, while their mind wanders far from the words of his prayer. As often, Luther may be guilty of caricature here, but he is again, in the process, trying to establish a new form of prayer, which combines the set liturgical forms with extempore simplicity, arising out of faith that prayer is heard by a loving father.

The reason why this identification of God as Father is vital for prayer is that only so can there be any degree of confidence that God will, in fact, answer our prayers. For Luther, prayer requires an expectation that it is no fruitless or pointless activity, so a vital issue is the grounds on which requests are made to God.

We know less than we would like about lay people's prayers in the late medieval period. There is written liturgical material, and of course the many Books of Hours available, but by definition, there is less evidence of more spontaneous, personal prayer. One example of the latter is a small personal prayer book profiled in an article by Peter Matheson.[27] This was a small collection of lay prayers in vernacular German belonging to Argula von Grumbach, who of course became a key figure in the spread of the Reformation in Bavaria in the 1520s, and who kept this book from her youth, perhaps because it illustrated the kind of prayer that the Reformation departed from. Especially notable is the fact that few of the prayers are addressed to God. Instead they are addressed to Mary, to 'one's own angel' (*zü seinen aigen engel*), and even to 'one's own twelfth apostle, or saint' (*zü seinem aygen zwelf potten*). When it comes to this question of the grounds on which prayer is offered, attention focuses on personal virtue, holiness and piety. The prayer to the 'twelfth apostle' asks: 'I beg you on the last day in the presence

---

[26]*LW* 42.23.
[27]Peter Matheson, 'Angels, Depression and "The Stone": A Late Medieval Prayer Book', *JTS* 48 (1997): 517–30.

of the heavenly emperor judge and lord of all the world to pray
for me and secure me such grace since I have lived so uprightly
and reverently on this earth and vale of tears, since I have served
almighty God so diligently and kept myself so sensibly from sins,
so that by the grace and mercy of almighty God I may also cheerfully and uprightly endure with your help the last judgement.' Here
is the classic synergism of late medieval spirituality – divine grace
and mercy are required, but only to aid human piety and virtue – it
is the soteriology of the *via moderna* in popular intercessory form.

If Luther's gospel focused on an external, not an internal, righteousness, finding value and confidence not in one's own goodness,
but in the goodness of Christ, then this shift can be seen in the practice of personal prayer. Luther insists that prayer is offered on the
basis of God's fatherly goodness, not on human virtue or goodness.
'Our prayer must not be based upon or depend upon our worthi-
ness or that of our prayer, but on the unwavering truth of the divine
promise ... We pray after all because we are unworthy to pray. The
very fact that we are unworthy and that we dare to pray confidently, trusting only in the faithfulness of God, makes us worthy to
pray and to have our prayer answered.'[28]

Here we come to the heart of Luther's teaching on prayer: that
it depends entirely on faith. It does not acquire merit before God,
nor does its efficacy depend on the piety, passion or urgency of the
petitioner, but it depends entirely on the grace and mercy of God.
The attention is shifted therefore from the pray-er to the one one
prayed to. Luther's version of prayer is an attempt to shift attention
away from an introspective spirituality that is constantly taking its
own temperature, seeking to stoke up its own fires into a pious
fervency, but instead is rapt in attention to a God who is gracious,
kind, eager to listen and hear, longing to hear our prayers more than
we are to pray. Prayer is thus quite simple: it is paying attention to
God, a focus of the mind and heart on him, and in the context of
that reassurance of his mercy and favour, a presenting of needs,
longings and requests.

There is a temptation in all prayer to assume that an answer
depends on something within ourselves, that God will listen to
prayers if we have been sufficiently pious, or are able to articulate

[28]*LW* 42.88–9.

eloquent or elegant prayers. Luther's emphasis on the merits of Christ, and the Fatherhood of God, is an indication that divine response is not determined by the eloquence of the prayer, the holiness or theological knowledge of the intercessor, but by something within the divine character itself, a willingness to listen to his children.

As might be expected with Luther, the way to approach prayer is not with confidence in one's ability to pray well or eloquently, or even contrition for sin, but with the faith that simply believes the promise that God listens to our prayers: 'It is necessary that we never doubt the promise of the truthful and faithful God. The very condition on which he promises fulfilment, yes, the reason he commands us to pray, is so we will be filled with a sure and firm faith that we will be heard.'[29]

Prayer is effective not because of any quality in the prayer itself, its eloquence, its seriousness or its fervency, but is in correlation to the faith that animates the prayer: 'Therefore, take note that a prayer is not good and right because of its length, devoutness, sweetness, or its plea for temporal or eternal goods. Only that prayer is acceptable which breathes a firm confidence and trust that it will be heard (no matter how small and unworthy it may be in itself) because of the reliable pledge and promise of God. Not your zeal but God's Word and promise render your prayer good.'[30]

If there is one word that characterizes Luther's approach to prayer, it is 'confidence'. The Small Catechism's teaching on the Lord's Prayer starts with this: 'God would encourage us to believe that he is truly our Father and we are truly his children in order that we may approach him boldly and confidently in prayer, even as beloved children approach their dear father.'[31] Luther's prayer breathes a confidence that avoids presumption precisely because the confidence in God hearing and responding overcomes the quality and frailty of a person's virtue, holiness or even their faith. The strength of the faith is not the issue; it is the simple question of whether God's gift of Christ and his coming to us as a heavenly father is trusted or not. This is to state the point positively. To

---

[29]*LW* 42.87.
[30]*LW* 42.77.
[31]Theodore G. Tappert (trans. and ed.), *The Book of Concord: The Confessions of the Evangelical Lutheran Church* (Philadelphia: Fortress Press, 1959), p. 346.

state it negatively and polemically, prayer indicates a willingness to distrust one's own wisdom. There is, in fact, a kind of dialectical relationship between Scripture and prayer for Luther. On the one hand, it is the promises of Scripture that reassure the Christian that prayer will be heard and is not a waste of time. On the other hand, prayer is needed to understand Scripture in the first place: it is vital to the theological task. In his Preface to the Wittenberg Edition of his Works of 1539, he outlines the nature of theology, seen as the exposition of and deep engagement with Scripture, as beginning with *Oratio*, and moving on to *Meditatio* and *Tentatio*: 'Firstly, you should know that the Holy Scriptures constitute a book which turns the wisdom of all other books into foolishness, because not one teaches about eternal life except this one alone. Therefore you should straightway despair of your reason and understanding. With them you will not attain eternal life, but, on the contrary, your pre-sumptuousness will plunge you and others with you out of heaven (as happened to Lucifer) into the abyss of hell. But kneel down in your little room and pray to God with real humility and earnest-ness, that he through his dear Son may give you his Holy Spirit, who will enlighten you, lead you, and give you understanding.'[32]

It is because Scripture brings us a strange wisdom, one that contradicts common sense and counters usual assumptions that it has to be approached in prayer, not with confidence in one's own rational, hermeneutical ability. Prayer is thus an expression of con-fidence in divine rather than human wisdom.

Unanswered Prayer

If faith is so central to prayer, is the fact that some prayers go appar-ently unanswered, due to a lack of faith, a deficiency in belief in the person praying? Luther has a number of things to say to this com-mon problem in prayer.

First, he advises against assuming that we know how God should answer our prayers. Intercession necessarily involves a certain reserve in how God will respond: 'Your trust must not set a goal for God, not set a time and place, not specify the way or the

---

[32]*LW* 34.285–6.

means of his fulfilment, but it must entrust all of that to his will, wisdom, and omnipotence. Just wait cheerfully and undauntedly for the fulfilment without wanting to know how and where, how soon, how late, or by what means. His divine wisdom will find an immeasurably better way and method, time and place, than we can imagine.'[33] We are to pray, confident that God hears our prayers, loves us and is working for our good, but how he will answer our prayers is entirely up to him. God may choose to work in hidden, secret ways, as indeed he did in Christ, hiding his divinity in and behind the human flesh of Christ, or in the sacraments, where the body and blood are hidden in, with and under the bread and wine.

This dynamic of prayer can be seen in Luther's response to one great crisis that Europe faced in his lifetime: the threat of the Turk. Towards the end of Luther's life, Islamic hordes seemed to be on the verge of invading and taking over Europe. The Ottomans had won the battle of Mohacs in 1526, and in 1541, the Hungarian city of Buda had fallen into Muslim hands, the Sultan turning the city cathedral into a mosque. It seemed only a matter of time until the rest of Europe would be taken over. In September of that year, Luther wrote his 'Appeal for Prayer against the Turks', as his response to this threat. Through this Turkish invasion, God was indeed teaching Christian Europe a lesson for their ingratitude and willful rejection of the gospel. However, besides repentance, the main response, certainly preceding any military riposte, should be prayer that believes God will hear: 'Whoever is inclined to doubt that God will answer his prayer might as well drop the idea entirely and not bother with God and prayer, for God cannot and will not tolerate our doubting.'[34] The argument that prayer is hopeless because God's predestined will is bound to happen is not to be entertained – that kind of fatalism is exactly how the Muslims themselves argue. The people are to pray, because they do not know what will happen and God's command is simply that we pray: 'We have to put this idea out of our minds and hearts and allow the future to be a hidden secret. We have to do what we know we ought to do according to God's word and the light he has given us.'[35] Yet how God is to answer prayer is

---

[33]*LW* 42.89.
[34]*LW* 43.231.
[35]*LW* 43.236.

entirely up to him: 'We should not determine the when and where and why, or the ways and means and manner in which God should answer our prayer. Rather we should in all humility bring our petition before him who will certainly do the right thing in accordance with his unsearchable and divine wisdom.'[36] Luther offers no suggestion as to how divine deliverance will come, but is content to leave the prayer at the level of pure entreaty and trust.

While he cautions reserve in prayer, making requests but not insisting on the particular ways in which God answers prayers, that does not exhaust Luther's response to the problem of prayers that seem ignored. From very early in his writings, he insists that often it is, in fact, spiritually advantageous when prayers are not apparently answered. In his commentary on Romans, written in 1516–17, he argues that when God answers prayers directly and straightforwardly, it sometimes simply confirms a person's sense that she knows what is best for her, and her own wisdom: 'It is not a bad sign, but a very good one, if things seem to turn out contrary to our requests. Just as it is not a good sign if everything turns out favourably for our requests. The reason is that the excellence of God's counsel and will are far above our counsel and will.'[37] Yet so often it is that very self-confidence and assurance of our own wisdom that need to be broken down.

Luther's *theologia crucis* dominates his thinking at this point in his theological development, and this teaching on prayer aligns closely with it. The Theology of the Cross says that God's first action with the sinner is his *opus alienum* of breaking down self-confidence – one's own sense of righteousness and goodness – through the experience of the cross, which means despair, doubt, temptation and the *Anfechtungen* that were part of Luther's own experience of the Christian life. Yet these are only preparatory for his *opus proprium*, his work of establishing a trust in the alien righteousness of Christ, received not by works or goodness, or the acquisition of merit, but by faith in Christ. Unanswered prayer, paradoxically more effectively than answered prayer, does exactly this by making the sinner go back to square one, realizing that his own desires and longings do not necessarily coincide with what God wants for him. God can sometimes only do this work of humbling and self-questioning

---

[36]*LW* 43.231.
[37]*LW* 25.364–5.

precisely by not giving us what we ask for. We can only receive what he wants to give us when he takes away what we cling to, when we find that our desires are not met and have to ask ourselves basic questions about what we asked for in the first place:

> Hence it results that when we pray to God for something, whatever these things may be, and He hears our prayers and begins to give us what we wish, He gives in such a way that He contravenes all of our conceptions, that is, our ideas, so that He may seem to us to be more offended after our prayers and to do less after we have asked than He did before. And He does all this because it is the nature of God first to destroy and tear down whatever is in us before He gives us His good things.[38]

God hears our prayer and responds. On one occasion in 1540, Philip Melanchthon, Luther's great friend and academic colleague, fell ill in Weimar. Luther prayed for his friend and he had, miraculously, so it seems, been healed. As he wrote to his wife, Katie, shortly afterwards: 'Philip truly had been dead, and really, like Lazarus, has risen from death. God, the dear father, listens to our prayers. This we can see and touch with our hands, yet we still do not believe it. No one should say Amen to such disgraceful unbelief of ours.'[39]

As we will see in Chapter 8, Luther had a heightened sensitivity to demonic activity all around him. The world is a battleground, with evil forces alive and active, seeking to contradict and frustrate the work of God. One of the major weapons in the Christian's armoury to defeat Satan is prayer. A week later, he writes again to Katie: 'Master Philip is returning to life again from the grave; he still looks sick, yet he is in good spirits, jokes and laughs again with us, and eats and drinks with us as usual. Praise be to God! You people, too, should join us in thanking the dear Father in heaven who raises the dead and who alone gives all grace and blessings; praised be he in eternity. Amen. But pray zealously, as you people ought to do, for our Lord Christ, that is, for all of us who believe in him,

---

[38] LW 25.365.
[39] LW 50.208–9.

[and pray] against the crowd of devils who now rage at Hagenau[40] and rebel against the Lord and his anointed.'[41]

There is an aggressive, urgent, insistent side to Luther's prayer: 'For prayer in my opinion is a constant violent action of the spirit as it is lifted up to God, as a ship is driven upward against the power of the storm ... For true prayer is omnipotent, as our Lord says: "For everyone who asks receives, etc." (Matt. 7:8). Thus we must all practice violence and remember that he who prays is fighting against the devil and the flesh.'[42]

Insistent confident prayer makes things happen. At other times, however, he draws back from suggesting that our prayers are the decisive factor. As he put it in a sermon on Matthew 6, we should pray 'certain that we are heard and that God knows what we need and intends to do it, even before our prayer'. Prayer is as much to do with changing us as changing God: 'We do not pray in order to teach God, but rather that we ourselves might be moved by our ills to perceive what we lack and what we should ask for. For it is myself to whom prayer teaches what I need, and myself whom it moves to pray and cry out.'[43]

Luther's reformation of personal prayer shared much with forms of mystical prayer, especially the demand for serious attention in prayer and the full, affective engagement of heart, mind, soul and body in the practice. At the same time, he was selective in what forms of traditional texts could helpfully be used, urging a blend of traditional forms with personal extempore prayer, which could be more extensively used the more mature and experienced the intercessor. He also aimed at a simplification of patterns of prayer. The primary focus was on addressing God as 'Father' – a Father who can be trusted to hear, listen and respond, and therefore a corresponding emphasis, not on the piety or eloquence of the prayer, but on the character of the one to whom prayer is addressed. Lutheran prayer was meant to be brief, personal and confident, sure that the

---

[40]The reference to Hagenau was to a forthcoming colloquy with papal representatives to work out a theological basis for Charles V's policy of reconciliation between opposing religious groups in the empire.
[41]LW 50.215–16.
[42]LW 25.460–1.
[43]LW 67.38.

Father hears the requests of his beloved people. As he reminded Peter Beskendorf:

> Finally, mark this, that you must always speak the Amen firmly. Never doubt that God in his mercy will surely hear you and say 'yes' to your prayers. Never think that you are kneeling or standing alone, rather think that the whole of Christendom, all devout Christians, are standing there beside you and you are standing among them in a common, united petition which God cannot disdain. Do not leave your prayer without having said or thought, 'Very well, God has heard my prayer; this I know as a certainty and a truth.'[44]

---

[44]*LW* 43.198.

PART C

Luther and the Christian Life

7

Luther on Sex and Marriage

It is surprising that Martin Luther had anything to say about marriage at all. He had, after all, two very good reasons not to know anything much about marital life – he had taken a double vow not to be married: when he joined the Augustinian order as a friar in 1501 and when he was ordained a priest in Erfurt Cathedral in 1507.

However, against all the odds, Luther married. It happened in June 1525, when Luther, aged 41, married Katherina von Bora, a 26-year-old former nun. The age difference was at some variance from Luther's own advice – he once gave the opinion that young men should marry at around 20, and young women between 15 and 18 years. Katharina was not a peasant; she came from a noble family, but had few great social connections. Her mother had died when she was quite young, and perhaps because of this, she had been given to a Benedictine monastery for her education at the age of five. When she was ten she had taken vows to become a nun in the Cistercian order.

In 1521, Luther had written a treatise 'On Monastic Vows', criticizing the idea of lifelong pledges that he believed bound people into unhealthy patterns of life and introverted community.[1] He had argued that vows ran counter to the Word of God, do not derive from faith or evangelical freedom, and offend against common sense and reason. For him, monastic life, of which he had a fair degree of experience himself, 'finds sin in matters of food, clothing, drink, laces, persons, works, acts, where Christ finds no sin, but commands that there be freedom in everything'.[2]

---

[1]'The Judgment of Martin Luther on Monastic Vows', LW 44.251–400.
[2]*LW* 44.398–9.

Partly as a result of this short book, monasteries and convents around Germany began to decline. More and more monks and nuns began leaving the cloister, feeling released from their vows by Luther's doctrine of evangelical freedom, and this was the fate of the small Cistercian convent at Nimbschen, where Katharina lived. A group of nine nuns from the convent had abandoned their vows, escaped from the monastery hidden in a cart laden with barrels of herring, and eventually arrived in Wittenberg, after an arduous journey of around fifty miles. The authorities in Wittenberg began to try to see how they could cater for these destitute women, which meant either returning them to their families or finding husbands for them. Eventually there was only one left unanswered for. Katharina could not return home, but was proving somewhat difficult to marry off. There was one suitor whom she quite liked but nothing came of it; another was proposed, but she rejected him resoundingly, finding him too old and cantankerous.

Until this point, Luther had always said that he was not interested in marriage. He always claimed that sexual desire was not a particularly great problem for him, perhaps because he had lived in a university since he was 17, and then in a monastery from the age of 21, both of which were all-male contexts, in which he seldom encountered women in any great intimate way.[3] He had been arguing against priestly monastic celibacy since 1520, but only in a very theoretical way. Most of his academic and clerical colleagues in Wittenberg were now married, partly because Luther himself had encouraged them to do so. Luther had teased his close friend and legal advisor Georg Spalatin, urging him to get married (which he did in 1525), only to find him returning the compliment by asking why Luther himself did not follow his own advice. A plan began to hatch among Luther's friends to sort out the problem of Katie, by urging him to marry her himself. Luther was not immediately attracted to her – he thought her too arrogant and strong-minded – but gradually the idea grew on him and he finally decided to marry. It was not a very romantic start – as he wrote to his friend Nicholas Amsdorf:

---

[3]See Lyndal Roper, *Martin Luther: Renegade and Prophet* (London: Bodley Head, 2016), ch. 13.

Indeed, the rumour is true that I was suddenly married to Katherine; [I did this] to silence the evil mouths which are so used to complaining about me. For I still hope to live for a little while. In addition, I also did not want to reject this unique [opportunity to obey] my father's wish for progeny, which he so often expressed. At the same time, I also wanted to confirm what I have taught by practicing it; for I find so many timid people in spite of such great light from the gospel. God has willed and brought about this step. For I feel neither passionate love nor burning for my spouse, but I cherish her.[4]

On 13 June 1525, Luther became formally engaged to Katie in the Augustinian monastery, in front of various friends who were witnesses to the event. The marriage service followed immediately. As was customary at the time, the couple were led to the bedroom and laid down before witnesses on the bed, which made their marriage vows binding. They then left the couple to their own devices, while the guests sang the night away outside. The public procession to the church for a blessing came a little later, as did the marriage feast that took place two weeks afterwards, on 27 June.

This, of course, was deeply controversial. Apart from the scandal of a man who was a monk and priest marrying, it was also extremely bad timing. The year 1525 was one in which the 'Peasants Revolt' had reached its climax. This was a large-scale, popular revolution of disenfranchised, alienated German artisans and peasants against their temporal and spiritual rulers, using the name of Luther as their inspiration – after all he had argued for the right of lay people to reform the church, that local parish clergy should be elected by the people rather than imposed by bishops and that the gradual infringements of the rights of the poor had to be stopped. Germany was convulsed with conflict, peasants were dying in the fields of Frankenhausen, the great battle that brought an end to the revolt in which 6,000 of the ramshackle army were slain, and here was Martin Luther getting married! He had already written what was called a 'Harsh Letter', urging the authorities to put down the rebellion, and now it seemed that all he was worried about was his own personal happiness, not the plight of the peasants. This played into

---

[4]LW 49.117.

the hands of the opponents of the Reformation, who claimed that it was all about sex and personal agendas. Rumours spread that he had got Katie pregnant, or that she had ensnared him by her female wiles, and his friends warned that he would be open to severe criticism if he went ahead. Luther, stubborn as ever, decided to carry on with the plan, partly to show that he was practising what he preached, but also, as he put it, simply 'to spite the devil'![5]

Despite all this, it was a remarkably successful marriage. Both were strong characters, had their fair share of arguments, but teased each other affectionately, and somehow the union worked remarkably well. Luther was a rather impractical and garrulous academic, welcoming guests, student lodgers and dinner companions into his home all the time, without much regard for how this was to be paid for on his relatively meagre salary. Katie, however, ran the house, did the accounts, managed the lodgers, even buying a nearby farm to grow produce for the family kitchen. They had six children, two of whom died young, and clearly held a deep affection for one another. She eventually died in 1522, six years after her husband.

Luther's views on marriage were quite distinct from those of many in his time. In the spiritual and ecclesiastical atmosphere in which he was brought up, being married was seen as an inferior spiritual state. To be a monk, or a nun, priest or bishop was a higher calling, and in each case it meant that marriage was no longer a possibility. In his several writings on marriage, Luther's reimagining of marriage in the light of the gospel reverses that order – to be married is the highest calling in the Christian life, superior to being a priest or a monk. As he explores this view, he highlights a number of key insights on marriage.

Marriage Is Pleasing to God

At a time when marriage was seen as an inferior state to single celibacy, the vital thing in marriage is to know the pleasure of God in it: 'One should not regard any state as better in the sight of God than the estate of marriage.'[6] Pre-Christian pagans (by which Luther

---

[5]*LW* 49.111.
[6]*LW* 45.47.

means the Greeks and Romans) thought that marriage was inevitably unhappy, that a wife was a 'necessary evil', but necessary to bear children.[7] The 'papists' say it is secondary to the primary callings to be a priest or a monk. Luther, on the other hand, addressing his readers, claimed that 'your life and conduct with your wives is the work of God and pleasing in his sight'.[8] Married couples are to remember that they are in a state pleasing to God. Monks or nuns never know whether their way of life is pleasing to God or not, as it never says explicitly in the Scriptures that it is, yet Scripture clearly says that to be married, to be a mother or a wife, a father or a husband is pleasing to God, and therefore is a higher calling than that of either monk or nun.

In fact, a couple need to be committed not just to their spouse, but also to the estate of marriage itself. There are times when a spouse may be irritated or frustrated by their partner, which is when it is vital to hold to the institution of holy matrimony, remembering that this estate is good and pleasing to God, even when the marriage is going through a difficult period. Luther is well aware that marriages can get dulled by familiarity and taught that even a difficult marriage is pleasing to God. Couples should not get divorced just because the wife or husband are at odds with one another. In fact, 'a successful marriage is a rare thing.'[9] The reason why married couples get bored with one another and start to be attracted to other people is because the devil opposes good marriages. There can be a restlessness in the human soul and within marriages that is never satisfied. The wise Christian never listens to the common weariness that can be found in marriage – that is just the devil's talk.

A husband or wife should see their spouse, whoever they are, and however difficult or easy they may be, as a gift from God. We think we choose our spouses, but in the deepest sense they are given to us by God rather than chosen by us. In marriage God gives the one to the other, and therefore husband and wife are to receive the other as a pure gracious gift rather than as a burden, or even a freely chosen partner. This perspective works perhaps better at a time of largely arranged marriages, but even then, it was presumably possible to resent one's spouse if one had had relatively little choice in the matter. For Luther, it was vital to see a spouse as much if not

---

[7]*LW* 57.226.
[8]*LW* 45.38.
[9]*LW* 45.17.

more chosen and given by God than by one's parents. In fact, God comes to a person in the guise of their spouse, so that it is possible to see the hand and face of God in this gift. Luther put it eloquently in a wedding sermon from 1531:

> God's word is actually inscribed on one's spouse. When a man looks at his wife as if she were the only woman on earth, and when a woman looks at her husband as if he were the only man on earth; yes, if no king or queen, not even the sun itself sparkles any more brightly and lights up your eyes more than your own husband or wife, then right there you are face to face with God speaking. God promises to use your wife or husband, actually gives your spouse to you, saying: 'The man shall be yours; the woman shall be yours. I am pleased beyond measure! Creatures earthly and heavenly are jumping for joy.' For there is no jewelry more precious than God's word; through it you come to regard your spouse as a gift of God and, as long as you do that, you will have no regrets.[10]

Sexual Desire Is Healthy

One of the most remarkable aspects of Luther's nuptial theology is his emphasis on sexual desire as something natural, normal and not to be shunned as inherently sinful. For Luther, 'the marriage bed is pure in the sight of God.'[11] Ever since Augustine's complex relationship with sexual sin had bequeathed an involved and convoluted relationship between the overpowering nature of sexual desire and the irrationality of sin, the Western church had always entertained a distinct fear of the power of libido. For Augustine, sexual desire was the perfect example of how sin operates – it is so overpowering that it overrides all other rational considerations in its wish to get the object of its desire. Sex was therefore always tied up with sin. As a result, it is perhaps not too much of an exaggeration to say that much mediaeval monastic spirituality was dominated by the fear of lust.

---

[10]WA 34.52, 12–21. Translation in Scott Hendrix, 'Luther on Marriage', in Timothy J. Wengert (ed.), *Harvesting Martin Luther's Reflections on Theology, Ethics, and the Church* (Grand Rapids and Cambridge: Wm. B. Eerdmans, 1984), pp. 169–84 (184).
[11]LW 51.365.

Luther believed that sex was still affected by sin, but not in the realm of desire. He located any potential sin in sexual desire in its tendency to be selfish, concerned more for the satisfaction of one's own physical impulses rather than the desires of the other. The desire itself is not intrinsically disordered.[12] Even married love is diminished and hindered by lust, a form of love that is more interested in satisfying one's own desire rather than pleasing the other. This is the opposite of married love that is focused on how one might please one's spouse. To this extent marriage is the kind of remedy for lust, a place where it can be redeemed and healed: 'Marriage is like a hospital for incurables, which prevents inmates from falling into greater sin.'[13] Lust can be handled rightly in the marriage bond, as the failure to love one's spouse, though sinful, can still be overcome by divine forgiveness. To this degree marriage, and the proper use of sexual desire, is only made possible, as Paul Hinlicky points out, by Christ.[14]

In his world, Luther observes two possible ways to deal with self-oriented sexual desire. One is what we might call casual sex, where neither really gives themselves to the other, and the act is only about personal individual pleasure. The second is repression, which is manifested in the call to monasticism. Those who try to suppress sexual urges by entering the monastery will only build their own frustration. The only proper response to the inevitable and divinely created urge for sexual fulfilment is marriage in which each gives themselves to the other. Lust is therefore channelled into a kind of love that is all about orienting oneself towards another person rather than being wrapped up in oneself.[15]

Sex within marriage is an obligation. The husband or wife has to give themself, body and soul, to their spouse. The sexual impulse is something God has ordained, and it will follow its course somehow.

---

[12]Aquinas, e.g. sees the purpose of genital organs as being purely to 'beget and educate offspring'. As every act that is not properly related to its requisite end is a disordered act, the implication is that sexual desire that is not necessarily related to procreation is intrinsically sinful. Thomas Aquinas, *On Evil* (Oxford: Oxford University Press, 2003), p. 421.

[13]*LW* 44.9.

[14]Paul R. Hinlicky, *Luther and the Beloved Community: A Path for Christian Theology after Christendom* (Grand Rapids: Eerdmans, 2010), pp. 201–9.

[15]It is worth recalling here Luther's famous definition of sin, the heart 'curved in upon itself' – *incurvatus in se*. Marriage is therefore a remedy for sin in that it turns the heart out towards another.

Priests, monks and nuns 'have no power by any authority, law, command or vow to hinder this which God has created within them. If they do hinder it, however, you may be sure that they will not remain pure but inevitably besmirch themselves with secret sins or fornication. For they are simply incapable of resisting the word and ordinance of God within them. Matters will take their course as God has ordained.'[16]

Luther believes, like Augustine, that sexual desire is overpowering, yet his response is not to tie sexuality closely to sin, but to enable it to find its proper outlet, through a positive theology of marriage. Sex is good created desire, and he implies it is not just a necessary means to produce children. It can be misdirected, but within the context of marriage it becomes something holy and delightful.

Luther, of course, always held a very physical theology. For him, unlike the more spiritualising Zürich reformer, Huldrych Zwingli, the bread and the wine of the Holy Communion, for example, could convey Christ's real, physical presence, hidden with and under the actual bread and wine given to the communicant. The water of baptism did really cleanse and renew. Luther never entertained the distaste for the flesh that his more spiritualist colleague in Wittenberg, Andreas Karlstadt, had. Sex was as natural as eating, drinking and defecating, and Luther was interested in them all.

It must be said that at times this emphasis on the inevitability of the sexual urge does lead him into strange territory. At one point he argued that sex was necessary because if semen is not issued from the male body it eventually turns poisonous, and the body becomes 'unhealthy, enervated, sweaty and foul-smelling'![17] However, his teaching on sexual desire sounded an unusual note in sixteenth-century writing on the topic and gave rise to a very different appreciation of sex and marriage in the Protestant world.

Sexual Difference Is Good

Luther draws a clear distinction between views of gender and sexuality in Christian theology compared to other schemes of thought.

---

[16]*LW* 45.19.
[17]*LW* 45.45.

Plato, for example, believed humanity was created androgynous and was then split into two. Aristotle, on the other hand, thought the woman a defective male. Luther, however, emphasizes God's creation of humanity as coming in two forms – male and female. This was not a secondary action of God, but his express desire from the beginning. In 'The Estate of Marriage', he writes:

> God divided mankind into two classes, namely, male and female
> ... This was so pleasing to him that he himself called it a good
> creation [Gen. 1:31]. Therefore, each one of us must have the
> kind of body God has created for us. I cannot make myself a
> woman, nor can you make yourself a man; we do not have that
> power. But we are exactly as he created us: I a man and you
> a woman. Moreover, he wills to have his excellent handiwork
> honoured as his divine creation, and not despised. The man is
> not to despise or scoff at the woman or her body, nor the woman
> the man. But each should honour the other's image and body
> as a divine and good creation that is well-pleasing unto God
> himself.[18]

Being male or female is not a matter of choice – it is something given. We have 'the kind of body God created for us'. Therefore Luther draws the conclusion that each should honour the opposite's body as a good creation. Although Luther can hardly be called a feminist in the light of his fairly conservative and wholly expected sixteenth-century views on the relationships between men and women in society and in marriage, he is an unlikely champion of gender equality in his absolute insistence that both male and female are the excellent handiwork of God.

The divine statement 'be fruitful and multiply' is not so much a command for Luther as an ordinance. In other words, it simply describes the way things are, rather than telling us to do something. We do not have to be told to multiply – we do it in the natural course of events. God creates us so that we have to multiply. Sex and gender are therefore not about commands but about ordinances. God does not command us to be male or female, or to multiply, but creates us so we have to do this. 'God does not command anyone to be

---

[18]*LW* 45.17.

a man or a woman.'[19] Gender is not an arena of conscious choice – whether or not to be what God has created a person to be, but part of a good creation to be received. Sexual difference is therefore both good and God-ordained as part of a good creation.

The implication of this is that women are not simply sexual temptresses for men, receptacles for male vice or distractions from the intellectual or spiritual life; they are divinely ordained and equally given partners to men. The papists, he says, despise women. They deny this good creation by the exaltation of celibacy and virginity. In fact, they would not create women if they had the choice![20] Luther still thinks of the husband as the head of household, and the wife has to obey, submit and respect her husband; however, his bold statement 'man and woman are the work of God' allows no disparaging of the other sex, or of marriage.

Marriage Depicts Salvation

In an early sermon of 1519, Luther repeats the traditional medieval view of marriage as a sacrament, a sign of something holy and eternal. Luther develops this sacramental theology in a direction taken by few other theologians. It is a picture of the gospel, in that it depicts God's gift of himself to us, body and soul. As we saw in the first chapter, Luther's theology revolved around the gift of Christ to us, which for him is not a mere spiritual offering but the incarnate Word, graciously offered to make us righteous. In the same way, it depicts our giving of ourselves to God, body and soul. As a result, marriage, this union of opposites, is a picture of the gospel, the mutual, exclusive and lifelong giving of God to us and us to God. In 'The Freedom of a Christian', his programmatic text of 1520 in which he laid out the heart of Christian faith, he had used the image of marriage as a picture of the gospel:

> The third incomparable benefit of faith is that it unites the soul with Christ as a bride is united with her bridegroom. By this mystery, as the Apostle teaches, Christ and the soul become

[19]LW 45.18.
[20]LW 51.359.

one flesh [Eph. 5:31–2]. And if they are one flesh and there is between them a true marriage – indeed the most perfect of all marriages, since human marriages are but poor examples of this one true marriage – it follows that everything they have they hold in common, the good as well as the evil. Accordingly the believing soul can boast of and glory in whatever Christ has as though it were its own, and whatever the soul has Christ claims as his own.[21]

Luther speaks of the marriage covenant in which through the 'wedding ring of faith' Christ takes our 'sins, death, and pains of hell which are his bride's' and gives us 'his righteousness in exchange'.[22] It also depicts salvation in that it is lifelong. Marriage is thus a kind of preaching of the gospel, a dramatic enactment of justification, in which the righteousness of the incarnate Christ becomes ours, and our sin becomes his. More than this, however, the union of difference between male and female is a sign of the union of the divine and the human natures in Christ – two natures in one flesh.[23] It also depicts salvation in that it is a lifelong exclusive commitment, a sign of God's commitment to us and ours to him. In marriage, 'by binding themselves to each other, and surrendering themselves to each other, the way is barred to the body of anyone else, and they content themselves in the marriage bed with their one companion.'[24] In just this way marriage is a sign of the call to worship God alone, with no wandering eyes or hands.

Luther, of course, eventually denied that marriage was a sacrament in the full medieval sense of the word. Only the Lord's Supper and Baptism fulfilled the criteria of being a command that was united with a physical sign as taught directly by Jesus. However, it is possible to see Luther's view of marriage as, if not a sacrament, certainly sacramental, in that it is such a clear and distinct picture of the reality of the Christian's relationship with God and of the incarnate Christ himself. In 1536 he preached at the wedding of his Wittenberg colleague Caspar Cruciger, in which he explicitly denied marriage was a sacrament. However, he still sees it as a mystery

[21]LW 31.351.
[22]LW 31.352.
[23]LW 44.10–12.
[24]LW 44.11.

pointing to something else. The Christian couple have the privilege of living in two estates: a physical marriage in flesh and a spiritual marriage with Christ. The marital state is an image and example of the love shown to us in Christ.[25] Christ the Son binds himself to us as our husband, a tie 'which is said of no other relationship or friendship'.[26]

However, as Luther points out, we do not see this. It takes an act of faith to see this hidden bond – that behind this external union of two individuals is the rich pattern of the divine economy. In fact, this is the hidden secret of every marriage. It is much more than the coming together of two people who decide to live together to bring them happiness, it is a sign of the central reality of life and salvation. On the surface, marriage appears like any ordinary relationship, such as friendship or a business partnership, but it is always much more than this. We are invited to believe that it is always a sign of something much greater – the union of Christ with the church and the believer. As he put it in a sermon in the Castle at Eilenburg in 1536: 'The marital state has been presented and depicted by God as an image and example of the high, inexpressible grace and love that He has shown and shared with us in Christ, as the most certain and lovely sign of the highest kindest union between himself and Christendom and all its members than which nothing closer can be imagined.'[27]

Marriage and Propagation

One of the primary purposes of marriage is to bring children into the world. To bear children, for Luther, is one of the highest Christian callings. 'The greatest good in marriage, that which makes all suffering and labour worthwhile, is that God grants offspring and commands that they be brought up to worship and serve him.'[28]

Christian couples are to bring up children to serve God, to praise and honour him. There is, in fact, no better thing a person can do for the church and for Christendom than bring up children well. It

---

[25]LW 57.232.
[26]LW 57.234.
[27]LW 57.232.
[28]LW 45.46.

is better than any pilgrimage, building churches, endowing masses for the dead: 'If we want to help Christendom, we most certainly have to start with the child.'[29] Parents are to be more concerned for the soul than for the body of their children. They are not heirs to be spoilt, but 'eternal treasures' to protect, and handled with the love that bothers to discipline and mould into healthy adults.

In his 1545 Marriage Sermon, Luther goes so far as to say that the purpose of marriage is to ensure the propagation of the human race, and in particular God's kingdom. The Christian calling is to 'live godly, honourable, pure and chaste lives, bearing children and peopling the world, indeed the Kingdom of God'.[30] This again is a distinct position taken up by Luther – that the purpose of marriage is to ensure that the kingdom of God is filled up! This conviction is so strong that he insists that apart from three categories, those who are 'eunuchs from birth',[31] those 'made eunuch' by men and lastly those who choose to be so and have the gift to remain single – a rare and social calling from God, all others should marry. Monastic vows are no excuse: 'Priests, monks and nuns are duty-bound to forsake their vows whenever they find that God's ordinance to produce seed and to multiply is strong in them.'[32]

For Luther marriage, and the setting it gives within which children can be born and nurtured into healthy, God-fearing, mature adults, is pleasing to God because it is the foundation of life: 'Without it, no man would exist.'[33]

The Impact of Luther on Views of Marriage

Some aspects of Luther's view of marriage sound distinctly strange to us today. Luther never really emphasizes the dignity of the single

---

[29]*LW* 44.13.

[30]*LW* 51.359.

[31]In a sermon on Matt. 19:10–12, Luther describes this: 'Toward women, they are like a hard rock, or a block of wood. A man is born a eunuch, just as someone has been born blind, so that he remains totally cold and indifferent to the female body.' *LW* 68.17.

[32]*LW* 45.19.

[33]*LW* 45.43.

life, as he is so keen to redress the balance that he felt was disturbed by the glorification of the celibate life in the monastic world. The sixteenth-century context of largely arranged marriages is also very different from today, making Luther's insistence that everyone should get married difficult to apply in the contemporary context.

Luther was often treated as a kind of judge in case of marital conflict, in which he often took a rather pragmatic view, for example, allowing women whose husbands were impotent to arrange (with his consent) a secret marriage with someone else (e.g. the husband's brother) to bear children, while the unfortunate husband retains the title to ensure he keep his property.[34] This seems strange advice to us, but perhaps it is testimony to how important the bearing of children was to Luther, as well as their value as potential heirs, in the context of property laws in early modern Europe.

On divorce, Luther recognized three valid grounds for divorce – impotence, adultery and a refusal of intercourse – though insisting at the same time that while these reasons can be valid in the secular realm, in the kingdom of God, Christians are urged to forgive such sins and move on.[35] It is, in his view, perfectly valid to marry a heathen or a Jew, a Turk or even a heretic, as all are God's good creation. While medieval canon law said that the blind or the dumb should not marry, Luther was perfectly content to say that they were perfectly entitled to form marital unions, as were cousins, and other family relations prohibited under medieval canon law.

Luther's rather flexible approach to marital advice got him into trouble in one particular instance when one of the most significant Protestant rulers, Philip of Hesse, asked for help with his own unhappy marriage in 1539. Phillip, in whom sexual desire, in contrast to Luther, always seemed to rage furiously, had fallen for a 17-year-old girl, whom he believed could satisfy his sexual urges in a way that his own wife, Christina, could not.[36] The girl's mother,

---

[34]*LW* 45.20–1.
[35]Contrary to a common misunderstanding of the Reformation, it did not make divorce any more possible than beforehand. See Susan C. Karant-Nunn, 'Reformation Society, Women and the Family', in Andrew Pettegree (ed.), *The Reformation World* (London: Routledge, 2000), pp. 433–60 (449).
[36]Philip complained about her lack of warmth, her consumption of alcohol and her smell. Nonetheless, the couple did have ten children, so she can hardly have been as bad as he made out!

however, had insisted that there could be no secret union, and that if he was to have his way, he had to marry young Margarethe. Philip could not divorce Christina, as she had always been faithful to him, and so he turned to Luther and the other reformers for advice. The Wittenbergers could not afford to alienate such an important political supporter, and so Luther and Melanchthon agreed to sanction a clandestine marriage with Margarethe, while Philip remained married to Christina, using the argument of polygamy as evidenced among the Old Testament patriarchs. They hoped that this endorsement of bigamy would remain secret; however, it soon came out, bringing a barrage of criticism Luther's way. He claimed that his advice had been dependent on it being kept secret – hardly a very principled stance, which convinced few – and he later privately admitted he had made a mistake. His advice can be seen as a conflict between two aspects of his teaching on marriage. On the one hand was his general belief in the natural and inevitable nature of sexual desire, which must be satisfied within the proper channels and structures. However, in this case such a conviction ran into conflict with his equally strong belief in the exclusive nature of the marriage bond as a picture of the relationship between Christ and the church.

For Luther, marriage was not just a spiritual arrangement, but 'an outward bodily thing, just like any other worldly undertaking'.[37] It was a secular undertaking, subject to temporal courts, but carrying a deeper theological meaning. The Reformation's treatment of marriage shows how in some way it contributed to the secularization of European life. The Reformation took many aspects of life out of the hands of the church and gave it to the secular power. It did this because it felt the church was either corrupt or had lost its focus on spiritual matters, transgressing the boundary between the two kingdoms, as Luther would have put it. In many Reformation cities, alongside taxation and social welfare, matrimonial law was taken out of the hands of episcopal courts, and placed under the jurisdiction of civil courts, never to return.[38]

---

[37]LW 45.25.
[38]See, e.g. the arrangements made in Strasberg and Ulm under Martin Bucer in Martin Greschat, *Martin Bucer: A Reformer and His Time*, trans. Stephen E. Buckwalter (Louisville: Westminster John Knox, 2004), p. 110.

Luther bequeathed a very different attitude to marriage in the Protestant world that emerged from the Reformation. It is sometimes argued that the Reformation replaced wider, more diffuse forms of family life with the birth of the nuclear family,[39] and there is certainly truth in the idea that the Reformation did reimagine family life, cutting away some of the quasi-familial relationships that abounded in medieval religious life. However, the Reformation ideal was not just the simple nuclear family, protecting itself from a wider hostile world. Luther's household, with numerous guests, students and visitors, gives a different picture, with the immediate simple family at its heart, and yet holding hospitality as a crucial virtue in familial life. The Protestant family at prayer was not just father, mother and children, but often included servants, house guests, relatives, neighbours and others, as it did in the former Augustinian Priory in Wittenberg, which became Luther's home.[40] The family became vital in a way it never was in medieval Europe. The household was seen like a small church. The family was not a sideline, an irrelevance to serious Christian existence that was primarily lived in the monastery, convent or church, but the primary vocation in which to live the Christian life.

At the heart of Luther's vision of marriage was a particular kind of love, which imaged the unique and pure love of God. In a sermon preached before he was married, he contrasted three kinds of loves. There is false love, which is the desire for things such as money, honour or selfish sexual pleasure. Then there is natural love, the normal affection for family and friends. And then there is married love, which desires just the beloved and nothing else. This kind of love 'glows like a fire, and desires nothing but the other person'. It says: 'It is you I want, not what is yours: I want neither your silver nor your gold; I want neither. I want only you.'[41]

This is the nature of divine love, which gives itself body and soul to the other. It is also a picture of the kind of love that divine love elicits in us – a love that is self-forgetful, forgetting one's own works, virtues or piety, and simply transfixed with a love for this God who gives himself to us, whose word can be trusted absolutely, engendering the desire simply to please him and no one else.

---

[39]Karant-Nunn, 'Reformation Society', pp. 433–9.
[40]See Alec Ryrie, *Being Protestant in Reformation Britain* (Oxford: Oxford University Press, 2013), pp. 363–405.
[41]*LW* 44.9.

8

Luther on the Devil

Luther was ordained a priest in the imposing Cathedral in Erfurt on 3 April 1507. The new priest was to celebrate mass for the first time a short while afterwards on 2 May. Friends were invited, as was his father who came with a large retinue from their home in Mansfeld. His father had been reluctant to agree to his son's calling, first to the monastery and subsequently to the priesthood, having had in mind a career for him as a lawyer, perhaps in the service of the emperor, perhaps helping sort out legal cases connected to his own family mining business.[1] As the day drew nearer, Luther found himself filled with foreboding at what he was about to do. To handle the very body and blood of Christ, into which the bread and wine were to be transformed, was such a breathtaking thing that Luther trembled in his spirit at the prospect.

During the service, facing the altar in the by-now familiar chapel of the Cloister of the Augustinian Friars in Erfurt, as he found himself uttering the words, 'We offer unto thee, the living and the true God … ', he suddenly faltered. As he put it later: 'Who am I, that I should lift up my eyes or raise up my hands to the divine Majesty? For I am dust and ashes, and full of sin, and I am speaking to the living, eternal and the true God!' He whispered his misgivings to the prior of the monastery who was assisting him, but as these were not unusual emotions for a new priest, especially one as scrupulous as brother Martin, he advised him to continue, nonetheless. These, however, were neither routine utterances of a feigned humility nor were they the paranoid fears of a psychologically disturbed

---

[1]This is an intriguing suggestion made in Lyndal Roper, *Martin Luther: Renegade and Prophet* (London: Bodley Head, 2016), p. 27.

neurotic. They were the natural and inevitable consequence of the medieval view of the mass, taken seriously. It may be hard for modern sensibilities to understand, yet given what he and his world believed about God, the awful judge of humankind, and given what medieval Christians believed about the mass, it is perhaps not surprising that a thoughtful and attentive student such as Luther would tremble at performing such an act.

The day still held one more dramatic turn. The service over, the new priest and the congregation retired to a separate room, where they were to celebrate with wine and rich food. Perhaps still shaken by his terrifying experience at the altar, and needing reassurance, he asked his father whether he was now reconciled to his son's entry into the monastery and ready to give his approval. Hans Luder, no longer able to hide his smouldering resentment, accused Martin in front of the guests of disobedience to his parents, leaving them to fend for themselves in their own age. Taken aback, Martin countered that as God had directly called him out of the thunderclap at Stotternheim, surely Hans should see this was God's will. 'God grant that it was not an apparition of the devil!' came the gruff reply.

Fifteen years later, the son admitted that his father's words 'penetrated to the depths of my soul and stayed there'.[2] This God whom he feared, the God who had apparently called him into the monastery, the God before whom he had stood trembling at his first mass – was he really the good God who he longed for him to be, the God of grace and kindness and mercy? Or was he, in fact, the devil – an angry, remorseless figure, dragging him through doubt, despair and self-torment, before picking up on the slightest excuse to damn him for all eternity?

God or Satan?

This question, of whether the God hidden in the mysteries of providence was, in fact, good and gracious, or secretly desired Luther's damnation, was an urgent and existentially fraught one in Luther's early development. His early theological searchings have been characterized as a search for a gracious God. David Yeago has pointed out how this phrase is, in fact, strangely absent form Luther's early writings, and suggests instead that Luther's question is: 'Where can I find the real God?'[3] The more urgent question was: what is God like? Who is the real God and is he good, or darkly indifferent?

That a divine figure existed behind the universe was hardly in question. The issue was the character of God, or his secret designs on humanity. Despite the suggestions of some scholars, it is unlikely that Luther, or any other sixteenth-century theologian for that matter, seriously entertained atheism as a realistic option. The main theme of Richard Marius's biography of Luther was that the reformer was dominated by the fear of death and the possibility that God might not exist.[4] He cites Luther's frequent references to death, alongside his comparative silence on the terrors of hell to argue the point. It is an intriguing suggestion, but ultimately fails to convince. Luther declined to speculate on the contours of hell not because he did not believe in them, but because it was precisely that – speculation. Despite the insistence (without much firm evidence) that such unbelief must have been widespread in the sixteenth century, there are few unambiguous indications that Luther struggled with atheism.

For Luther, 'unbelief' meant not atheism but a lack of faith in the word of God. Luther's fear was not so much annihilation as God himself. What if the God who condemns through the law, who assaults believers with *Anfechtungen*, the inscrutable hidden God who seems to damn sinners to hell, is the only God there is? In other words, what if God turns out to be the devil? In his famous account of his 'breakthrough' in the introduction to his German Works in 1545, Luther wrote: 'I did not love, yes, I hated the righteous God who punishes sinners, and secretly, if not blasphemously, certainly murmuring greatly, I was angry with God.'[5] If atheism is not an option, and there is someone lurking behind the created world and the events of providence, then the disturbing question is whether that person is good or evil. This is why his discovery of a

---

[3]David S. Yeago, 'The Catholic Luther', in Carl E. Braaten and Robert W. Jenson (eds), *The Catholicity of the Reformation* (Grand Rapids and Cambridge: Wm. B. Eerdmans, 1996), pp. 13–34 (17).
[4]Richard Marius, *Martin Luther: The Christian between God and Death* (Cambridge, MA: Harvard University Press, 1999).
[5]LW 34.336–7.

gracious God in Christ was so significant. In Christ he finds a God he can love, a God who is gracious, kind and merciful. However, it remains true to say, as Gerhard Forde does, that for Luther, 'apart from Jesus, God is indistinguishable from the devil.'[6]

God and Satan are sometimes hard to tell apart: 'The knowledge of God can ... be so pictured as if it is God's will to be angry, and one may be led to believe that our Lord God and the devil are both intent on strangling us.'[7] The devil can often be pictured by Luther as God's agent. He can speak of the 'devil and God's judgement' in the same breath.[8] This is because, as we saw in Chapter 4, God works his salvation by bringing the sinner through the experience of temptation, doubt and despair, which feels exactly like the assault of Satan, so much so that they are hard to distinguish. Yet this is only God's '*opus alienum*', his strange work to bring the sinner to the point where she despairs of her own goodness and piety, and instead trusts the Word that promises righteousness and life – God's proper work – his '*opus proprium*' – which is given in Christ. The experience of the devil's attacks and divine judgement may be identical, or as two sides of the same coin, but they are distinguished by their aim and goal. As Paul Althaus put it: 'Both (God and Satan) launch a heavy attack against man. God, however, does it to save and drive him into God's merciful arms. Satan does it in order to tear a man completely and finally loose from God ... One does it to save him, the other to put him to death.'[9]

The key to this dilemma is Christ. In Christ, God is gracious and kind, and desires salvation and mercy. God's true desire is revealed precisely in Christ and the Word that speaks of him, so the Christian is able to discern the different trajectories of divine and demonic work through clinging to the word that tells him that God

---

[6]Gerhard O. Forde, *The Captivation of the Will: Luther vs. Erasmus on Freedom and Bondage* (Grand Rapids and Cambridge: Wm. B. Eerdmans, 2005), p. 45.

[7]*LW* 54.34, No. 252.

[8]E.g. *LW* 14.28: 'The devil or God's judgment will reveal those sins that man cannot recognize or know.' The same idea is related often in this passage, Luther's Commentary on Ps. 117.

[9]Paul Althaus, *The Theology of Martin Luther*, trans. Robert C. Schultz (Philadelphia: Fortress Press, 1966), p. 167. A similar point is made by Hans Schwarz, *True Faith in the True God: An Introduction to Luther's Life and Thought* (Minneapolis: Augsburg, 1996), pp. 75–9.

is gracious. Luther tells of how the devil 'turns the Word upside down'.[10] However, rather than believing the demonic word that declares 'God says you are damned because you don't keep the law', the Christian is instead to respond: 'God also says that I shall live. His mercy is greater than sin, and life is stronger than death. Hence if I have left this or that undone, our Lord God will tread it under foot with his grace.'

God and the devil are locked in a battle for control of the world, the church and the creation, a battle in which the participants are often confused. Luther's preoccupation with the devil is complex and takes time teasing out, precisely because the devil's work is devious and deceptive. In what remains of this chapter, I try to outline the contours of Luther's view of the devil and why he was so preoccupied with the evil one.

Obsessed by the Devil?

The Wittenberg Reformer believed he was familiar with the devil's ways: 'I know the devil well', he says.[11] There are certainly times when to modern ears Luther sounds decidedly credulous, in that he shares common medieval beliefs in minor devils to be found in forests, woods and swamps.[12] Luther famously and frequently attributed the work of his enemies to the work of the devil, seeing satanic work behind all his opponents, whether the pope, the enthusiasts or the Turks.[13] At times, he seems so preoccupied with the devil that he veers into language that gives too much credit to satanic power. For example, speaking of the Two Kingdoms in his 'Bondage of the Will', he writes:

---

[10]*LW* 54.106, No. 590.

[11]*LW* 49.230.

[12]E.g. in a Table Talk of 1532: 'The devils, too, are very near to us. Every moment they are plotting against our life and welfare, but the angels prevent them from harming us. Hence it is that they don't always harm us although they always want to harm us ... There are many demons in the woods, water, swamps, and deserted places who may not injure people. Others are in dense clouds and cause storms, lightning, thunder, and hail and poison the air.' *LW* 54.172.

[13]For an account of these controversies, see Mark U. Edwards Jr, *Luther's Last Battles: Politics and Polemics, 1531–46* (Ithaca: Cornell University Press, 1983).

For Christians know there are two kingdoms in the world, which are bitterly opposed to each other. In one of them Satan reigns, who is therefore called by Christ 'the ruler of this world' and by Paul 'the god of this world'. He holds captive to his will all who are not snatched away from him by the Spirit of Christ, as the same Paul testifies, nor does he allow them to be snatched away by any powers other than the Spirit of God, as Christ testifies in the parable of the strong man guarding his palace in peace. In the other Kingdom, Christ reigns, and his Kingdom ceaselessly resists and makes war on the kingdom of Satan.[14]

All of this has led many to critique Luther for an obsession with demonic activity that becomes virtually dualist.[15]

Of course, Christian theology has never held that the devil is the evil counterpoint to God. The devil is not an uncreated power alongside God – that was always a heretical view held on the margins of mainstream Christianity by groups such as the Manichees and, nearer to Luther's own time in early medieval Europe, the Cathars. Instead, the devil is a created being, an angelic servant who did not want to serve, and instead rebelled against God, as the story is told in many strands of European literature, from Dante Alighieri to Edmund Spenser to John Milton.[16]

Yet the question remains as to why Luther was so obsessed with demonic activity and powers especially in his later life, and whether the accusation of dualism actually sticks. Such an enquiry means trying to understand what lies behind his 'theology of evil', if we can speak of such a thing, and his understanding of demonic power and its work in the world.

---

[14]*LW* 33.287.

[15]E.g. Richard Marius: 'The quest for demonic forces was for Luther only the obverse of his quest for God. If the one did not exist, the other did not exist either, and all meaning in life fell to earth and ashes.' *Martin Luther*, p. 478.

[16]There are hints of this in Old Testament texts such as Isa. 14:12–15, Ezek. 1:28. The fall of the angels becomes a larger theme in Intertestamental writings such as the Wisdom of Solomon, and 1 and 2 Enoch, a tradition that is never explicit in the NT, but is reflected in texts such as Lk. 10:18: 'I saw Satan fall like lightning from heaven', and 2 Pet. 2:4: 'God did not spare the angels when they sinned, but cast them into hell and committed them to chains of deepest darkness to be kept until the judgment.'

Satan Opposes the Work of God

God is the only one who creates. Yet Luther is keenly aware that his work is opposed within the world, and by more than human powers. Luther shares the belief of most of his contemporaries that Satan is a fallen angel, who fell through the sins of pride and jealousy.[17]

Satan's work is therefore to undo the work of God. 'God loves life. The devil hates life.'[18] The devil has no creative power. All he can do is destroy, and seek to reduce the world to the emptiness and nothingness from which it came: 'God ... raises the dead, gives life to the dead, and calls into existence the things that do not exist. The devil can destroy what has been made, but he cannot rebuild it. He can also consume a house with fire, but he cannot make it rise anew from the ashes.'[19] This destructive work is focused in two areas – as we have seen in previous chapters, Luther often takes a dialectical view of the world and this is no less true of his theology of evil, as the devil seeks to undermine God's work in both the sphere of faith and the sphere of society.

Luther's gospel, as we have seen, centred on the external, alien righteousness of God, given to us in Christ, and to be received by faith alone. The response God desires is not activity, works, holiness or piety, but simple trust – this is the heart of divine work in the soul. Yet because God's work is always opposed, the aim of Satan is to attack faith in Christ. It is to make a person believe that God is not good, that Christ died for others, but not for him, that God's word of promise cannot be trusted, that he has to somehow earn the favour of God through acquiring merit and so on. It is to oppose the gospel. Luther sees the original sin of Adam and Eve, the sin that opened the door to the entry of evil, suffering and

---

[17]'The devil was a very handsome angel and a decidedly outstanding creature. But when he saw that it had been predetermined that God would assume human nature and not the nature of the angels, he was inflamed with envy, anger, and indignation against God for not being willing to take him, who was a most handsome spirit, and for not being able to become a participant in the divinity and in such great majesty. It pained him that that wretched mass of human flesh had to be preferred to himself; for he thought that all this became him better than it did this sinful flesh, which is liable to death and all evils.' *LW* 5.221.

[18]*LW* 54.34.

[19]*LW* 22.247.

sorrow into the world primarily as Satan enticing them, not to the sin of disobedience, but of unbelief: 'First of all, the devil attacks their faith by telling them to give up this Word and not to regard it as God's Word. He is not interested primarily in the bite into the forbidden apple; it is his concern to lead them from faith, in which they were walking before God, into unbelief, from which disobedience and every other sin would necessarily follow as fruits.'[20]

Heiko Oberman called Satan, as Luther saw him, the 'master of subjectivity',[21] constantly seeking to persuade the Christian to trust her feelings of what seems or appears to be true, rather than the objectivity of God's promise given in Christ. Baptism and the Lord's Supper are objective guarantees, God's pledge that he is with us and for us in the battle against Satan. The devil therefore is the enemy of faith, inveigling us to put our trust anywhere but in Christ.

He also is the enemy of community. Luther has a strong sense of the order of the world, an order displayed in his classic teaching on the three structures that uphold social life: the household, the secular government and the church. The work of Satan in opposing the work of God is his activity to undermine all three of these structures. When these fall, social life falls and God's good ordering of the world breaks apart. This explains why Luther sees in his enemies not just human power at work, but also demonic forces lurking behind them:

> Against this rule of God, however, Satan rages; for his sole purpose is to crush and destroy everything that God creates and does through this rule. First he opposes the rule of God and, as far as God permits him, throttles and destroys and spoils everything that God creates, preserves, and improves. For he is the prince of this world, yes, even a god; in opposition to the rule of the angels he has his own angels, who inspire, counsel, and incite the princes, lords, and all men to nothing but evil and promote all hindrances to good and all furtherance to evil, incite the people against one another, set things aflame wherever they can, and fill the world with grief and heartache. Opposed to the spiritual rule he has the heretics, false teachers, hypocrites, false brethren;

[20]LW 24.343.
[21]H. A. Oberman, *Luther: Man between God and the Devil* (New Haven: Yale, 1989), p. 227.

and he does not rest until he has destroyed this rule. Opposed to the secular rule he has the rebellious, lawless scoundrels, evil, venomous counsellors at the courts of the princes, flatterers, traitors, spies, tyrants, madmen, and everything that promotes war, discord, and destruction of lands and people.[22]

Because he believed that heresy and false teaching undermined the church, that social unrest and warfare undermine peace and stability in society, and that adultery, neglectful parenting and family discord undermine the household, Luther sees a pattern in all these things that is more than accidental. A worldly pope, rebellious peasants and bad parents all serve to shake the foundations of good social order that is the divine will for life together. Hence he saw in all these something more sinister than mere social trends and cultural change: he saw an undoing of God's good creation. Luther's preoccupation with satanic activity is therefore not purely social but also political. It is motivated by a fear of the breakdown of social order, and to that extent is a manifestation of Luther's social conservatism.

These two attempts, to destroy faith and to undermine society, are the devil's real works, far more sinister than mere ghosts or ghouls. In one particularly vivid reminiscence, Luther recounts how

it is not a unique, unheard-of thing for the Devil to thump about and haunt houses. In our monastery in Wittenberg I heard him distinctly. For when I began to lecture on the book of Psalms and I was sitting in the refectory after we had sung Matins, studying and writing my notes, the Devil came and thudded three times in the storage chamber as if dragging a bushel away. Finally, as it did not want to stop, I collected my books and went to bed. I still regret to this hour that I did not sit him out, to discover what else the Devil wanted to do. I also heard him once over my chamber in the monastery. But when I realised that it was Satan, I rolled over and went back to sleep again.'[23]

Luther's writings are full of reports of such incidents, strange happenings, bumps and bangs in the night. However, the remarkable

---

[22]LW 20.173.
[23]WA TR 6, No. 6832; 219.30–40, translation in Oberman, Luther, p. 105.

thing about Luther's reaction is the shrug of the shoulders when he decides that these strange noises are the devil – that is nothing compared to the real work of the devil in opposing faith and threatening salvation and social order.

Dealing with the Devil

This leads us directly to the question of how Luther advised confronting the devil's attacks. The heart of Luther's belief about the devil can be seen ultimately by looking at how he recommended Christians tackle satanic activity directly. The very sin of Satan was precisely that he claimed to be on a par with God, as Luther says: 'Lucifer presumed to be God's equal'[24] or 'Satan always wants to be God's mimic and ape, but God hates him.'[25] Although Luther's writings, especially towards the end of his life, are full of references to the devil, the devil is always under the hand of God, because he, like all angelic beings, is ultimately a creature. Luther even calls him 'God's Satan'. Thus, despite his preoccupation with the devil, which sometimes appears almost manic, and despite his language when speaking of the Two Kingdoms, Luther is not ultimately a dualist, believing that the world is split into two realms, one ruled by God and the other by Satan. He knows that while Satan rages, he still comes under God's power and authority.

When this belief is translated into the tactics of spiritual battle, Luther's main stratagem was laughter: 'Let us laugh at raging Satan and the world.'[26] Although, on the one hand, Luther takes Satan with the utmost seriousness as the enemy of God, life and all that is good, on the other, the great mistake is to take him as seriously as if he were God's rival. Satan's great sin and, at the same time, his great flaw is pride, and the one thing that the proud do not like is to be laughed at. Luther suggests seeing Satan as really nothing more than a small jumped-up creature who thinks he is as important as God, but is ultimately and, literally, ridiculous. He needs to be treated with disdain, not the disdain that fails to recognize the seriousness of his work and the extent of his influence, but a scorn

---

[24]*LW* 32.81.
[25]*LW* 16.17.
[26]*LW* 12.25.

that refuses to countenance his claims to be taken as seriously as God. Luther has a particular and characteristically crude way of dealing with the devil:

> I resist the devil, and often it is with a fart that I chase him away. When he tempts me with silly sins I say, 'Devil, yesterday I farted too. Have you written it down on your list?' ... Thus I remind myself of the forgiveness of sin and of Christ.[27]
>
> Almost every night when I wake up the devil is there and wants to dispute with me. I have come to this conclusion: When the argument that the Christian is without the law and above the law doesn't help, I instantly chase him away with a fart.[28]

Behind the menace, there is something comical about the devil and his pretensions. So the best strategy is to laugh at him. When Luther considers his opponents who write against him, he sees, as always, the wiles of Lucifer lurking beneath, and he begins to relax: 'while I sit under the shade of faith and the Lord's Prayer, laughing at the devils and their crew as they blubber and struggle in their great fury'.[29] This also explains much of Luther's crude and frankly foul language, especially about the devil. Luther often resorts to language of excrement, vomit, piss and wind to describe the work of Satan. It can sound just like the re-emergent rantings of Luther's rude peasant upbringing, yet such language does have a purpose of placing the devil where he belongs, revealing him for who he truly is. As Heiko Oberman says: 'A figure of respect, be he Devil or pope, is effectively unmasked if he can be shown with his pants down.'[30]

Luther's instinct is to recognize the work of the devil in all activity that opposes the creative, salvific will of God, to recognize the havoc he sees to make, but not to take him seriously at all, and instead to assert even human authority over him. In response to a story of a man whose home was invaded by the activity of a poltergeist, Luther counsels him not to worry at all about the flying kitchen utensils, but to banish the devil with the confidence of faith:

---

[27]*LW* 54.16, No. 122.
[28]*LW* 54.78, No. 469.
[29]*LW* 41.185.
[30]Oberman, *Luther*, p. 109.

Dear Brother, be strong in the Lord and firm in your faith! Don't give in to that robber! Suffer the outward things and the minor damage that comes from the breaking of pots, for it can't harm you in body and soul, as you have found, for the angel of the Lord is with you. Let Satan play with the pots. Meanwhile pray to God with your wife and children [and say], 'Be off, Satan! I'm lord in this house, not you. By divine authority I'm head of this household, and I have a call from heaven to be pastor of this church. I have testimony from heaven and earth, and this is what I rely on. You enter this house as a thief and robber. You are a murderer and a scoundrel. Why don't you stay in heaven? Who invited you to come here?' In this way you should sing him his litany and his legend and let him play as long as he pleases ... I was often pestered [by the devil] when I was imprisoned in my Patmos, high up in the fortress in the kingdom of the birds. I resisted him in faith and confronted him with this verse: God, who created man, is mine, and all things are under his feet. If you have any power over him, try it![31]

It is not just that God has Satan under his feet, but humans also are in true authority over Satan as a fallen angel, so part of the proper response is to stand on human dignity, asserting human authority over the works of the devil in the name of Christ. This captures much of Luther's way of dealing with Satan – to be always watchful, but to laugh him out of court.

The second way Luther suggests dealing with the devil is through prayer. The work of God is opposed aggressively, so Christians needs to respond aggressively, not passively. Luther never counsels physical violence in the name of Christ, but envisages a distinctly violent form of prayer. Luther always believed that military or legal force was useless in dealing with matters of faith. Crusades, the burning of heretics, the drowning of witches or forcing people to believe in a particular way was a waste of time. The Christian cannot go to war in the name of the Kingdom of God. Instead, prayer and testimony were the weapons of the Christian in the spiritual battle:

[31]*LW* 54.280, No. 3814.

For prayer in my opinion is a constant violent action of the spirit as it is lifted up to God, as a ship is driven upward against the power of the storm.... . This violence decreases and disappears, to be sure, whenever the Spirit draws and carries our heart upward by grace, or surely, when a present and major anxiety compels us to take refuge in prayer. And without these two factors, prayer becomes a most difficult and tedious thing. But its effect is tremendous. For true prayer is omnipotent, as our Lord says: 'For everyone who asks receives, etc.' Thus we must all practice violence and remember that he who prays is fighting against the devil and the flesh.[32]

The kind of prayer that drives out Satan is not gentle, contemplative meditation, but urgent, violent entreaty. While there is a place for quieter forms of prayer, there remains the need for active, purposeful prayer as a weapon of choice against the wiles of evil. At the same time, the mark of such prayer is faith, or, put differently, confidence that God hears the prayer and that it is sufficient to cast out the devil:

Satan seeks everything that is evil. Therefore we, on the other hand, must pray that everything that is evil may be warded off. God wants to pour out His goods with a full hand if only there were people who prayed and asked with confidence. Accordingly, our hearts must be inflamed with confidence. When confidence animates prayer, great violence is inflicted on the devil.[33]

In the face of satanic attack, the best recourse is to confident, pugnacious prayer: 'Satan is opposed to the church ... the best thing we can do, therefore, is to put our fists together and pray.'[34]

The third strategy that Luther recommends is Christian fellowship. Despite his own use of the tactic of farting to chase the devil away, Luther counsels caution in using this trick. He reminds his hearers of a woman in Magdeburg who banished the devil by breaking wind, but says it is only to be used carefully, as Satan is not easily expelled in this way. The devil does not always respond well

---

[32]*LW* 25.460.
[33]*LW* 30.281.
[34]*LW* 54.94, No. 518.

to such treatment, so handling the attacks of Satan need to be done not as an individual but as part of the church: 'No man should be alone when he opposes Satan. The church and the ministry of the Word were instituted for this purpose, that hands may be joined together and one may help another. If the prayer of one doesn't help, the prayer of another will.'[35] The place to do battle with Satan is firmly within the church, with its assurances of God's grace in the sacraments, the Word and the companionship of friends.

Conclusion

Recent scholarship has seen a renewed interest in Luther's Apocalypticism and his consequent preoccupation with the devil as raging extra hard because his defeat is near.[36] Luther's tendency to see the devil behind anyone who disagreed with him certainly made argument almost impossible. He also shared some medieval beliefs in demonic activity in nature that are hard to translate into the modern world. Towards the end of his life, his growing sense of gloom and disappointment over the progress of the Reformation tended to drive him at times to what seems a greater preoccupation with the devil and his works than with God. However, it would be a mistake to discount his teaching on Satan and the power of evil too quickly.

Heiko Oberman's classic biography focused on Luther 'Between God and the Devil', and argued that this aspect of his thought was not an unfortunate medieval remnant that clung to him despite his leanings towards the modern era, but was an essential part of his view of the world: 'Luther's world of thought is wholly distorted and apologetically misconstrued if his conception of the devil is dismissed as a medieval phenomenon and only his faith in Christ retained as relevant or as the only decisive factor. Christ and the Devil were equally real to him: one was the Intercessor for Christianity, the other a menace to mankind till the end.'[37] Luther's

---

[35]*LW* 54.78 No. 469.
[36]Much of this stems from Heiko Oberman's groundbreaking biography of Luther, originally published in German in 1981: *Luther: Mensch Zwischen Gott Und Teufel* (Berlin: Severin und Siedler, 1981).
[37]Oberman, *Luther*, p. 104.

theology is one that takes the reality of evil and all that threatens human life, society and the created order seriously, and to excise his awareness of demonic action within the world from his view of it is to emasculate his theology, to render it tame. Arguably, only a theology that takes evil seriously can speak to a world in which evil is so often apparent and rampant. A theology that fails to look it in the eye can say nothing in the face of terror, lethal acts of violence and destruction.

Furthermore, this means for Luther not just an impersonal principle of evil, but evil personified into the person of Satan. Creation is good, and the implication of that central Christian belief is the conviction that evil is not present in the world because of any flaw in the created order, like a potter who made a pot with a barely perceivable crack, which sooner or later was going to break the vessel into pieces. According to the tradition that stretched back to Augustine and beyond, evil enters the world due to an act of *will* on behalf of part of that Creation, which opposes itself to God. Only persons can exercise will, so that evil, however it manifests itself, requires a personal dimension. This is the kind of reasoning that has led Christian theology towards belief in a personal rather than an impersonal force of evil, and it is reasoning that Luther shares.

Luther's obsession with the devil, if we can call it that, is part of the radically dialectical nature of his theology. It is what makes him a theologian who can look despair, temptation, doubt and death in the face, knowing they are all opposed to the work of God and are his deadly enemies. However, it is ultimately dwarfed by his realization of the ultimately ridiculous and derisory nature of Satan's pretence to equal God. When enquiring about the nature and character of God, we need to learn to close our ears to the deceptive voice of a purely natural theology that highlights our experiences of the absence of God, and the presence of suffering, to conclude that God either does not exist or, if he does, that he is the monster of recent atheistic attacks on Christianity. Instead, we are to listen to the voice of Christ whose word stands over against the deceptions of Satan. Satan is simultaneously to be taken seriously but not listened to, recognized but not respected, disdained and not desired. It sometimes takes wisdom and faith to tell the difference between what appears to be God and the Devil, but the key to that wisdom is Christ.

9

Luther on Freedom

For Luther, one the most important results of the gospel of Christ's righteousness, received by faith, was the gift of true freedom. The years after the publication of the 95 Theses in 1517 saw a series of tense and increasingly charged exchanges, with representatives of the Papal church all trying to argue this truculent German monk into submission. None of them succeeded. In fact, each one drove Luther to express himself in more and more extreme ways. In 1520, with his name now famous (or notorious) across Europe, and the prospect of excommunication looming on the horizon, he wrote three treatises that in many ways were the defining documents of the Lutheran Reformation. The first, 'On the Babylonian Captivity of the Church', was a stinging critique of the stranglehold that the Papacy had put around the European Church. The second, 'To the Nobility of the German Nation', was an appeal to the lay leaders of Germany to rise up and reform the church, if the clerics were not going to do it. The third, the most famous and effective of them all, was titled 'On the Freedom of a Christian'. It was to be one of the most influential expositions of Christian liberty ever written.

At the time Luther was in the eye of the storm. His other writings of this period are full of furious accusation, defence and argumentation. Strangely, at this moment of gathering clouds and impending doom, this piece is a pool of tranquillity, an eirenic piece of writing that breathes peace, delight and security. He was so pleased with it that he claimed it 'contains the whole Christian life in a brief form, provided you grasp its meaning'.[1] Freedom is also one of the key issues in contemporary debates about society and anthropology

---

[1] *LW* 31.343.

and Luther's insights may have much to say to us today about how we understand and articulate a Christian view of freedom.

Christian Freedom

Luther's treatise starts with a bold statement that neatly encapsulates the paradox of freedom:

A Christian is a perfectly free lord of all subject to none.

A Christian is a perfectly dutiful servant of all, subject to all.[2]

To explain what he means by this, Luther makes a distinction that is crucial to his argument, between the outer and the inner person. This is a distinction that is often misunderstood. Luther does not have in mind a dialectic between some kind of inner self and a person's outward physical appearance, a Platonic dualism of body and soul. Rather, the distinction is a relational one: the 'inner man' is the human person as oriented towards and relating to God, and the 'outer man' is the human person oriented and related towards other people. The 'outer man' is therefore human life seen in social terms. In relation to God, each individual stands alone, unable to rest on anyone else's merits or faith. However, in society, we are inevitably social beings, drawn from the very outset into relationships. As is often thought, Luther is one of the architects of modern individualism, but only in relation to God, not in relation to others in society.

The 'inner man', the part of human life that is oriented to God, is nourished by the Word of God that assures him of God's love, grace and favour, a message that can only be responded to by a faith that trusts that the promise can be relied on. This faith is a truly powerful thing for Luther. It renders works redundant in establishing this relation to God, it honours God because it ascribes to him the worship and trust that he is due, and unites us with Christ in a unity that is as close as, if not closer than, that between a bridegroom and a bride. Rather than an insignificant figure burdened and restricted by sinfulness and inferior status,

---

[2]*LW* 31.344.

which severely limits his options and freedom to roam and to act, the Christian is a king, exercising authority over all things, with all the freedom that such a status brings, and moreover a priest with rights of access to the very presence of God himself. Freedom, for Luther, therefore, exists primarily in this realm, the realm of the 'inner man', in relation to God. It is very definitely an inner freedom, the freedom from fear or anxiety that anything can ultimately harm the Christian who trusts God. It is the freedom from sin and its power, the freedom to be and to do good. This, of course, does not mean that such a person is free of trials. In fact, 'The more Christian a man is, the more evil, sufferings and deaths he must endure, as we see in Christ ... and the Saints.'[3] However, such things cannot affect his inner freedom, his relationship to God, due to the strict line Luther draws between these two worlds. In this inner realm, there is the freedom of a clear conscience and a restful heart, freedom from any human rules, demands and burdens laid on the sensitive conscience.

This is the most fundamental and basic form of Christian freedom. It is ultimately, for Luther, the only freedom that counts, because it is freedom before God himself. The question then comes: how is this freedom to be used or exercised? This is when he turns to the 'outer man'. The person thus freed from sin, anxiety and fear devotes his freedom to serve the other, not because he has to, but because he delights to do so:

> From faith thus flow forth love and joy in the Lord, and from love a joyful, willing, and free mind that serves one's neighbour willingly and takes no account of gratitude or ingratitude, of praise or blame, of gain or loss. For a man does not serve that he may put men under obligations. He does not distinguish between friends and enemies or anticipate their thankfulness or unthankfulness, but he most freely and most willingly spends himself and all that he has, whether he wastes all on the thankless or whether he gains a reward.[4]

This voluntary chosen service is not over against freedom, as if it were a kind of compensation, a necessary balance in case we think

---

[3] *LW* 31.354.
[4] *LW* 31.367.

ourselves too free, it is an expression of freedom. It remains free because it is freely chosen, not compelled. If love and service were somehow necessary for salvation, they would become a burden, imposed from outside, not really feely chosen but basically done because we have to. Moreover, they become acts that are not truly acts of love. If a person's motive in an act of generosity is not ultimately to bless the other person through the gift, but really to gain personal merit, to win their own salvation or, as we would tend to put it in our own day, to look good, then it is not really an act of generosity at all. Only if the act is performed entirely freely, without the need for any personal reward, does it become a genuine act of love and honest service.

The distinction between inner and outer is strict, but it is not the case that they have nothing to do with each other. Inner freedom has implications for outer life. Precisely because of this inner freedom, the Christian freely chooses to become the servant of others. Having received this freedom as a gift from God, she gives her freedom as a gift to others. The outer self requires the exercise of certain disciplines so that the outer body conforms to the prior and more basic inner reality of freedom. If the body is not ordered and disciplined, it falls out of line with the inner reality, and fails to reflect it: 'In this life he must control his own body and have dealings with men. Here the works begin; here a man cannot enjoy leisure; here he must indeed take care to discipline his body by fastings, watchings, labours, and other reasonable discipline and to subject it to the Spirit so that it will obey and conform to the inner man and faith and not revolt against faith and hinder the inner man, as it is the nature of the body to do if it is not held in check.'[5]

All the time, Luther is keen to stress the distinction that disciplines, actions or works do not in themselves bring about freedom – only the Word of God, received by faith, does that. In the context of late medieval Christianity, a great deal of resources, effort and religious activities were put into ensuring personal salvation. Pilgrimages, indulgences and masses for the dead all sucked up vast resources of money and time. Luther's radical claim that such things achieved nothing in the realm of salvation

---

[5]*LW* 31.358–9.

suddenly released a huge amount of energy, time and money that could now be used to serve the poor and the neighbour. As Brian Gerrish put it: 'The liberation of a man from constant anxiety about the condition of his soul is what makes him available to his neighbour.'[6]

Two points can be made of Luther's vision of freedom here. The first is that, for Luther, freedom is a sheer gift. It is grace. It does not come about as a result of reward for services rendered to God, or as a right demanded from him – it is a gift that gives inner liberty, regardless of outward circumstances.

The second point is that because this freedom is a gift, it creates relationships. The Christian, free of the fear of sin, guilt, death and all the hosts of Satan, chooses to dedicate her freedom not to self-indulgence and to pleasure, but to the neighbour, because this freedom has been given as a gift. The gift creates a sense of gratitude and a kind of free obligation, a freely chosen service. This gratitude then issues in a renewed use of this freedom, exercised communally, not individually. Whereas other visions of freedom, such as the libertarian tradition, associated with figures such as John Locke and J. S. Mill, separate us from others in a privileged space of private liberty, making the 'other' a potential enemy who threatens my personal space and freedom of action, this vision of freedom creates relationships, in that this inner freedom is actively given to the other. There is for Luther a direct link between inner freedom and the outer use of that freedom as given to the other, and the link is the concept of freedom as a gift. As Luther says: 'I will give myself as a Christ to my neighbour, just as Christ offered himself for me.'[7] A Christian lives not in himself, but 'in Christ through his neighbour through love'.[8]

These are the beginnings of Luther's view of Christian freedom: Freedom as a gift, given by God and received by faith alone, which then, by virtue of its sheer gratuitousness, evokes a corresponding giving up of freedom, to become the 'perfectly dutiful servant of all'.

---

[6]Brian A. Gerrish, *The Old Protestantism and the New: Essays on the Reformation Heritage* (Edinburgh: T&T Clark, 1982), p. 89.
[7]LW 31.367.
[8]LW 31.371.

Freedom and Bondage

This was a positive, enticing vision of freedom. However, it also had its negative, polemical side. As Gerhard Ebeling put it: 'No theologian – we may even go further and say no other thinker – has spoken in such compelling terms of the freedom of man on the one hand, and with such terrifying force of the bondage of man on the other.'[9] Back in 1518, when he had appeared at a theological disputation in the University of Heidelberg, Luther had written: 'Free will after the fall, exists in name only, and as long as it does what it is able to do, it commits a mortal sin.' This was one of Luther's most controversial early statements that was picked up and condemned by the papal bull, which threatened Luther with excommunication, and which reached him in October 1520, just over a month after he had published 'The Freedom of a Christian'. For Luther, if the human will was active, trying to contribute something to salvation, then by definition, it cannot receive it as a gift. In fact, we commit sin by trying to earn something that was meant to be given as a gift. Luther had insisted from early on in his break from medieval soteriology that when it comes to salvation, we contribute nothing. Even faith is not a 'thing', an action we perform, it is merely the passive trust that holds on to the promise of God that offers justification, forgiveness and freedom.

This negative aspect of his view of freedom took a more controversial and polemical turn in 1525. By now, his break from the Roman church had taken place, and Luther was already set on a trajectory towards establishing a new form of church life. Before long, his idea of freedom came into conflict with one of the few comparably famous figures in European intellectual life: Desiderius Erasmus.

Luther and Erasmus had a good deal in common. They had both been educated in the movement known as the Brethren of the Common Life, were well-known reformers who denied the value of Aristotle's influence on medieval theology, disliked the Scholastic method and opposed the practice of Indulgences. Both valued the Bible, the study of its original languages and advocated reform

---

[9]Gerhard Ebeling, *Luther: An Introduction to His Thought*, trans. R. A. Wilson (London: Collins, 1972), p. 211.

by the laity. Their early exchanges had been friendly and mutually admiring. However, as Luther's own language become more extreme after his break with the papacy, Erasmus grew impatient with his younger fellow reformer. Erasmus, the cool, detached Renaissance man, began to be annoyed by the fiery Teutonic passion of Luther's rhetoric.

Erasmus also disliked Luther's dim estimation of human abilities and powers. He thought Luther's insistence that humankind could do nothing to contribute to their salvation, and could only believe in the promise of God extended to them, was demeaning to the dignity of humanity, something vital to a humanist like Erasmus.

Provoked into taking on Luther by none other than Pope Adrian himself, as well as by the accusation that was beginning to circulate, that as he had not written against Luther, he must be his supporter, in September 1524, Erasmus published *De Libero Arbitrio*, 'A Discourse on Free Will', directly attacking Luther's idea that justification comes by 'faith alone', and what he considered Luther's dogmatic and aggressive tone, particularly on the issue of the human will.[10]

An obvious corollary of Luther's idea of freedom as a free gift, to be received by faith, was the idea that without faith, there is no freedom. In fact, free will is a fiction. Erasmus wanted to claim some space for human action, arguing that if humans were not capable of responding to God's commands, then, on the one hand, salvation would seem arbitrary and, on the other, an important plank of morality would crumble. If there is no free will, who will ever make any moral effort at all? Who will reform their life? For Erasmus, the message that we are simply bound, with no wriggle room at all, no capacity to do anything in response to God, is a recipe for moral laziness. At the same time Erasmus simply wanted Luther to calm down. His was never a dogmatic position (he was, after all, never a dogmatic person), he only wanted Luther to tone down his rhetoric and admit some small space for human action, especially as this was not a cardinal issue of faith, and was not very clear in the Scriptures anyway.

---

[10]He had originally wanted to write a dialogue between a Lutheran, his opponent and an arbitrator, a casual, ruminatory discussion that would have been calmer, but probably a format unsuited for the heated nature of the debate that became necessary.

Luther replied with characteristic confrontational directness just over a year later, titling his response *De Servo Arbitrio*, 'On the Bondage of the Will'. The writing veers between respectful disagreement, withering critique and robust polemics. Its terminology is not always very exact and sometimes confusing,[11] but the main outlines are clear.

The same distinction between inner and outer man as we saw in his earlier 'Freedom of a Christian' remained implicit behind the discussion. With regard to 'outer' things – life in society – there is a degree of freedom. This is the realm of 'things below us', ordinary decisions of life such as what to have for breakfast or what clothes to wear. In this realm there is genuine though limited freedom to choose and to act. In the realm of 'things above us', the inner man, the realm of our relationship to God, however, there is no freedom of the will at all. And this is no 'obscure doctrine' as Erasmus suggested it was – it went to the heart of the gospel:

> I praise and commend you highly for this also, that unlike all the rest you alone have attacked the real issue, the essence of the matter in dispute, and have not wearied me with irrelevancies about the papacy, purgatory, indulgences, and such like trifles (for trifles they are rather than basic issues), with which almost everyone hitherto has gone hunting for me without success. You and you alone have seen the question on which everything hinges, and have aimed at the vital spot.[12]

This was life and death. Everything hinged on it. Luther pulled no punches: 'Here, then, is something fundamentally necessary and salutary for a Christian, to know that God foreknows nothing contingently, but that he foresees and purposes and does all things by his immutable, eternal, and infallible will.'[13] Here we hit on one of the most rigorous arguments for the absence of human freedom since Augustine's work over a millennium beforehand.

---

[11]Paul Hinlicky writes of the 'shoddy imprecision of Luther's terminology': Paul R. Hinlicky, *Luther and the Beloved Community: A Path for Christian Theology after Christendom* (Grand Rapids: Eerdmans, 2010), p. 156.

[12]*LW* 33.294.

[13]*LW* 33.37.

Why then does Luther see this as such a vital issue? Luther builds up a number of arguments that contribute to the same aim: to undermine any confidence in human independence from God, which he sees as the basis of free will.

First, he argues that free will is something only properly ascribed to God. God alone is free to choose without any restriction on his choice, with nothing external to him that influences his choice. That much he has learnt from his nominalist tutors in Erfurt. However, this has a consequence when it comes to human choice. Breaking from his nominalist education, he claimed that the inevitable corollary of this was that humans have no free will with regard to God. At the end of the day, either God or we have free will – we cannot both have it. If we did, they would come into conflict and that is logically impossible. God's choice to save us would come into conflict with our desire not to be saved, for example. Either God obeys and does what we want him to, or we obey and do what God wants us to – you cannot have both. There cannot be two free wills.[14]

Second, building on this point, he argues that God's will must prevail, otherwise God's promises cannot entirely be trusted. For Luther, salvation rests wholly on the promise of God. As he put it in 'The Freedom of a Christian': 'The promises of God give what the commandments of God demand and fulfil what the law prescribes so that all things may be God's alone, both the commandments and the fulfilling of the commandments.'[15] God gives his grace and goodness to us as a gift in Christ, and the appropriate response to a gift is simply to accept it. The appropriate response to a promise is just to believe it. Moreover, if God's promise is to be fulfilled, the only way we can be sure of it is if there is absolutely no question that it can be honoured. In other words, if some events are outside God's control, then that leads to doubt as to whether his promise will ultimately be kept:

For if you doubt or disdain to know that God foreknows all things, not contingently, but necessarily and immutably, how can you believe his promises and place a sure trust and reliance on them? For when he promises anything, you ought to be

---

[14]See Robert W. Jenson, 'An Ontology of Freedom in the *De Servo Arbitrio* of Luther', *Modern Theology* 10:3 (1994): 247–52.
[15]*LW* 31.349.

certain that he knows and is able and willing to perform what he promises; otherwise, you will regard him as neither truthful nor faithful, and that is impiety and a denial of the Most High God. But how will you be certain and sure unless you know that he knows and wills and will do what he promises, certainly, infallibly, immutably, and necessarily?[16]

For Luther, only necessity preserves the trustworthiness of the promise of God.

Third, any concession to human free will brings salvation into doubt. If salvation rests even just a little on human activity – some slight human action, as Erasmus wants to claim it must – then this too brings salvation into doubt. Questions inevitably arise – am I capable of what is being asked of me? Have I done enough for salvation? Is my contribution what is required? This is exactly the kind of fear that Luther had been delivered from in his original break from the soteriology of his contemporaries in the theological world of late medieval Christianity, and it is easy to see that Luther did not want to go back to that spiritually debilitating uncertainty.

Fourth, and here we come closer to the nub of Luther's argument, introducing human free will into the relationship between God and humankind paradoxically limits our freedom rather than establishing it. Erasmus had argued from morality, that unless there is some human free will to obey God's commands, no one would bother to make any moral effort. The problem with this, as Luther delights to point out, is that Erasmus actually becomes the theologian of the law, envisaging a heteronomous law set over against the human will. Our supposed human freedom to choose thus comes up against a barrier, a command that tells it what to do. It finds itself opposed, restricted, confined by the law that stands as demand over against it. The human will is no longer free to do as it wants, but is ordered to obey against its true inner desires. In this dynamic, the hidden, secret pull of sin, whether gossip, envy, pride or lust, has to be sublimated, suppressed, but never quite dealt with. Luther, on the other hand, sees no need for the law in the realm of salvation, thus envisaging the soul as free from the law and its demands. The will is only set free by the Word of God, which declares it forgiven,

---

[16]*LW* 33.42.

pardoned, justified. Paradoxically, by emphasizing human free will, Erasmus ends up as the theologian of bondage, and Luther, by emphasizing bondage, ends up as the theologian of freedom![17]

The only alternative to this is to allow no law at all, which leaves the human will enslaved to its own desires, and this takes us further into the heart of Luther's argument. His conviction is that free will is actually a fiction. It is a chimera, a fantasy that does not really exist. Why does he say such an apparently outrageous thing? Luther is reacting against the kind of thinking on freedom associated with the name of philosophers such as William of Ockham.[18] For Ockham, freedom of choice is paramount. The human will is radically free, and is dictated to by nothing and no one. Like the divine will, you cannot get behind human free choice to anything prior that dictates or forces it. The human will is not defined, as it was for Augustine and Aquinas, as attraction towards the good, originally designed as oriented towards God and goodness. It is alone in its lofty freedom.

Ockham's idea of 'free will' implied a perfectly balanced will, free from any external influence whatsoever. In a famous image, Luther depicts the human will like a horse that is ridden by one rider or another – either God or the devil.[19] The two riders fight for control, and the way the horse faces is determined by which rider has the reins. Luther's contention is that our wills are not entirely free to choose, as Ockham thought they were. We are at the play of forces outside ourselves. We deceive ourselves that we are in charge, but this is a fiction. We say that we do what we want, but that is exactly the problem – we are bound to do what we want, and what we think we want is swayed by things other than our own will: 'People are slaves to whatever masters them' (2 Pet. 2:19).

Only God has the kind of will that is entirely free of external influences. Human wills cannot just choose to change themselves – we cannot choose what to choose. And what we choose is not

---

[17]See Gerhard O. Forde, *The Captivation of the Will: Luther vs. Erasmus on Freedom and Bondage* (Grand Rapids and Cambridge: Wm. B. Eerdmans, 2005), ch. 2.

[18]Luther's early intellectual training was in the nominalist school of philosophy currently in the University of Erfurt, under his tutors Joducus Trutvetter and Bartholomäus Arnoldi von Usingen. For the best study of late mediaeval Nominalism, see Heiko A. Oberman, *The Harvest of Medieval Theology: Gabriel Biel and Late Medieval Nominalism* (Cambridge, MA: Harvard University Press, 1963).

[19]*LW* 33.66.

ultimately under our control. If you are suddenly overtaken with a
desire for chocolate ice cream, to go swimming or to tell a lie to get
out of trouble, you cannot simply choose to 'turn off' that desire.
You can try to suppress it if possible, but then you are effectively
curbing your freedom to act according to your wishes, which Luther
always points out is a kind of hypocrisy, doing one thing that you
secretly desire and thinking another. We are unable to change our
desires, as they are fundamental, and those desires are pulled one
way or the other by forces external to the self. As Paul Hinlicky puts
it: 'There is no freedom of desire; the will, taken as desire, spontaneously and necessarily seeks what appears good to it and flees
what appears evil. This capacity is what Luther has in mind when
he denies that the will can move itself, that is, cause itself to desire
something.'[20] To change the metaphor, free will is like a car in neutral
gear, unable to do anything. It only moves when it is put by a driver
into one gear or another, at which point it is no longer neutral – it is
fully engaged, either to advance or to go in reverse.

To use another image, Erasmus's idea of free will seemed to
imagine a moment on the scale between willing God's will and not
willing it, where the will is perfectly balanced and free, leaning neither to the one nor the other. The problem is that the will is always
drawn one way or the other, like a finely balanced see-saw that is
leaning one way, and once it reaches the tipping point, automatically leans over towards the other side. There is no moment when
it is perfectly balanced horizontally – it leans either one way or
the other.

The idea that the human will is free – in other words, perfectly
balanced and free to choose its own course of action, completely
independent of any external influence – is a fantasy. As Ebeling
says: 'The will is always already decided, involved and committed,
and is not the natural will in the situation of absolute freedom of
choice, the will considered in purely unhistorical terms. The will is
only the free will to the extent that it is able to do what it wishes.'[21]
The idea that we act uninfluenced by external factors is an illusion;
our decisions are always swayed by desires, moods, arguments, per-
suasions and enticements from outside, which determine what we
think we choose far more than we realize.

---

[20]Hinlicky, *Luther and the Beloved Community*, p. 157.
[21]Ebeling, *Luther*, p. 220.

This is a basic difference of anthropology from Ockham. Ockham thinks the will is primary and can shape our desires. Luther thinks that is psychological and theological nonsense. His is a more Augustinian anthropology that says desire comes before will. Our desires shape our thinking, not the other way round. We are lovers before we are thinkers, as James K. A. Smith has more recently put it: 'We are essentially and ultimately desiring animals, which is simply to say that we are essentially and ultimately lovers.'[22] And if God is the Creator who created us for himself, then we are either drawn to him as we were created to be or running away from him to try to establish our own freedom, which is no freedom at all, because it leaves us captive to any old whim that takes over our pliable and easily led hearts from the outside.

Captivated into Freedom

Luther's writing is always bold and brash. His doctrine of freedom starts with a conviction that freedom is not a right that can be demanded, nor something deserved or earned – in fact, such doctrines of freedom tend to set up a gap between desire and action, giving no good reason for acts of goodness or building social life, leaving the soul isolated in their freedom, with no reason other than a reluctant obedience to heteronomous law, to create social bonds. Freedom instead is a gift that creates rather than destroys relationships, first a free relationship of trust with the God who is the giver of freedom, because the means by which the gift is received is precisely by faith, which is the bond that unites us to Christ, the giver of freedom: 'Faith ... unites the soul with Christ as a bride is united with her bridegroom. By this mystery, as the Apostle teaches, Christ and the soul become one flesh.'[23] It then creates a social bond with others, in that it frees the sinner from anxiety about his own salvation and releases him for relationships with those around him in acts motivated by genuine love for the other, not for a selfish desire for personal salvation: 'A man does not live for himself alone in this

---

[22]James K. A. Smith, *Desiring the Kingdom: Worship, Worldview and Cultural Formation* (Grand Rapids: Baker Academic, 2009) pp. 50–1.
[23]*LW* 31.351.

mortal body to work for it alone, but he lives also for all men on earth; rather, he lives only for others and not for himself.'[24]

It has to be said that this argument perhaps works better in the context of sixteenth-century Europe where anxiety about salvation was a common experience; however, there are some important themes for our broader discussion about freedom here.

For Luther, the bondage of the will is not mere determinism as it is for Zwingli, and in some versions of later Calvinism. It is more like an addiction, in that we do what we are bound to do: 'We all do what we want to do! That is precisely our bondage.'[25] This is the freedom of the addict to take a drug. No one forces him to, he is not made to by some external law, but he takes it anyway. He feels free to do as he chooses, but in reality we know he has no choice. Put more positively, we might imagine being in love. We do not coolly sit down and choose what or who to love; instead we are captivated by the vision of someone or something, and that love then dictates our actions: 'The will cannot change itself and turn in a different direction ... Ask experience how impossible it is to persuade people who have set their heart on anything. If they yield, they yield to force or to the greater attraction of something else; they never yield freely.'[26] This is not some psychological erasure of the will, imagining human beings as robots, or automata who just do what they are programmed to do. There is an element of willing, but the will follows the pull of a powerful attraction. As Heinrich Bornkamm put it, Luther 'does not mean psychological compulsion but posits the necessity of a higher order that guides the will from above, no matter how spontaneously it may act'.[27]

The *Libero Arbitrio* that Erasmus had in mind seemed to envisage a perfectly balanced will, free to choose its own object of love. Luther's point is that this is theologically and anthropologically untrue – it is observably false from human experience as much as it does not accord with Christian theology. This is why Luther roots the bondage of the will not so much as a postlapsarian state, but as rooted in our created nature: this is a basic disagreement

[24]*LW* 31.364.
[25]See Forde, *The Captivation of the Will*, p. 37.
[26]*LW* 33.64–5.
[27]Heinrich Bornkamm, *Luther in Mid-Career* (London: DLT, 1983), p. 450. See ch. 16 for a detailed and extended discussion of this debate.

on anthropology. Humans are loving creatures. We act when we are captivated by something outside ourselves. The big question is: what captivates us? God? Or something more sinister? The entry of sin into the picture just complicates it. If there were no sin, we would still be enraptured, but only by God. The fact of sinfulness opens up the possibility of being enraptured by something pernicious: by our own selfish desire, or even by Satan himself. If our vision and desire is not captivated by God and goodness, it gets captivated by something else. As Gerhard Forde puts it: 'Unless the Spirit of God enters into the matter, the will goes badly.'[28]

In Christ, the divine Word that proclaims God's purpose to be gracious and kind, we find something that truly captivates us. It gives us a God we can love, and a God who captivates us into freedom, so to speak. Robert Jenson asks the obvious question: why are we delivered into freedom when God captivates us, and not when we are captivated by Satan, or by anyone else for that matter? The answer is that it is because God is the only One who is truly free, in the sense that he is not subject to any external force; his will is not determined by anything outside himself, but is entirely in control of his own will and desire. So, when God enraptures us, we are enraptured into his freedom. When Satan or anyone else captivates us, they cannot draw us into freedom because they do not possess it themselves. Only God can give us freedom, because he is the only one who possesses it. He is enraptured by nothing external, but only by himself, in the Trinitarian logic of the Father and the Son enraptured in love in the Spirit. 'Human freedom in the only sense Luther wants to talk about, is nothing less than participation in God's own triune rapture of freedom.'[29]

God's freedom, as Luther suggested when he expounded the Freedom of the Christian in 1520, is the freedom to give ourselves to each other in love, not because we have to, compelled by some external law, not because we are pre-programmed to, but because we are freed to do so, released from the self-serving requirement (in medieval terms) to acquire personal merit for salvation, or (in our terms) to impress others, prove ourselves or establish our sense of self-worth and goodness by doing good things. This is the freedom of what Hinlicky calls the Holy Spirit-inspired 'ecstatic selfhood

---

[28]Forde, *The Captivation of the Will*, p. 55.
[29]Jenson, 'An Ontology of Freedom', p. 252.

of faith',[30] the self that is liberated from self-interest and obsession, and thus free for the neighbour. Building on Luther's insights,
though put a little differently to how Luther would express it, a
Christian vision of freedom imagines people released from the pull
of destructive desires, not to leave them stranded with an arbitrary
free will, perfectly poised and free to choose either good or evil (as
Erasmus had suggested), but captivated by a vision of a good, kind
and gracious God who draws them into relationships of love, inter-
dependence and delight, which are exactly the kind of relationships
we find at the heart of God himself.

---

[30]Hinlicky, *Luther and the Beloved Community*, p. 169.

BIBLIOGRAPHY

À Kempis, Thomas. *The Imitation of Christ*. Glasgow: Fount, 1977.
Althaus, Paul. *The Theology of Martin Luther*, translated by Robert C. Schultz. Philadelphia: Fortress Press, 1966.
Bell, Theo. *Divus Bernhardus: Bernhard Von Clairvaus in Martin Luthers Schriften*. Veröffentlichungen des Instituts für Europäische Geschichte Mainz, vol. 148. Mainz: P. von Sabern, 1993.
Bernard of Clairvaux. *Opera Omnia*, J. P. Migne (ed.), Patrologiae Cursus Completus Series Latina, vol. 182. Paris, 1879.
Bernard of Clairvaux. *The Works of Bernard of Clairvaux*, translated by Killian Walsh. Kalamazoo: Cistercian, 1976.
Bluhm, Heinz. *Martin Luther: Creative Translator*. St Louis: Concordia, 1965.
Bonaventure. *The Soul's Journey into God*. Mahwah, NJ: Paulist Press, 1978.
Bornkamm, Heinrich. *Luther in Mid-Career*. London: DLT, 1983.
Braaten, Carl E. and Robert W. Jenson (eds). *Union with Christ: The New Finnish Interpretation of Luther*. Grand Rapids: Wm. B. Eerdmans, 1998.
Bray, Gerald (ed.). *Documents of the English Reformation*. Cambridge: James Clarke, 1994.
Brecht, Martin. *Martin Luther: His Road to Reformation, 1483–1521*, translated by James L. Schaaf. Philadelphia: Fortress Press, 1985.
Brecht, Martin. *Martin Luther: Shaping and Defining the Reformation, 1521–1532*, translated by James L. Schaaf. Minneapolis: Fortress Press, 1990.
Brecht, Martin. *Martin Luther: The Preservation of the Church, 1532–1546*, translated by James L. Schaaf. Minneapolis: Fortress Press, 1999.
Calvin, John. *Calvin's Commentaries on the Book of Psalms*, translated by J. Anderson. Edinburgh: Calvin Translation Society, 1844.
Calvin, John. 'Treatise on Relics'. *Tracts and Treatises on the Reformation of the Church*. Edinburgh: Oliver & Boyd, 1844.
Calvin, John. *Calvin's Commentaries on the Twelve Minor Prophets*, translated by J. Owen. Edinburgh: Calvin Translation Society, 1847.

Calvin, John. *The Institutes of the Christian Religion,* John T. McNeill (ed.), Library of Christian Classics, 2 vols, translated by Ford Lewis Battles. Philadelphia: Westminster John Knox, 1960.

Calvin, John. *The Acts of the Apostles,* translated by T. H. L. Parker, vol. 6; Calvin's New Testament Commentaries. Edinburgh: Oliver & Boyd, 1966.

Carr, D. M. S. 'Consideration of the Meaning of Prayer in the Life of Martin Luther'. *Concordia Theological Monthly* 42:9 (1971): 620–9.

Chillingworth, William. *The Religion of Protestants.* London: Bell & Daldy, 1870.

Damerau, Rudolf. *Die Demut in Der Theologie Luthers,* Studien zu den Grundlagen der Reformation, vol. 5. Giessen: Schmitz, 1967.

Davies, J. G. *Pilgrimage Yesterday and Today: Why? Where? How?* London: SCM, 1988.

Ebeling, Gerhard. *Luther: An Introduction to His Thought,* translated by R. A. Wilson. London: Collins, 1972.

Edwards, Mark U., Jr. *Luther's Last Battles: Politics and Polemics, 1531–46.* Ithaca: Cornell University Press, 1983.

Elze, Martin. 'Das Verständnis Der Passion Jesu Im Ausgehenden Mittelalter Und Bei Luther'. In Kurt Aland, Walther Eltester, Heinz Liebling and Klaus Scholder (eds), *Geist Und Geschicte Der Reformation: Festgabe H. Rückert.* Berlin: Walter de Gruyter, 1966: pp. 127–51.

Erasmus. 'Enchiridion'. In M. Spinka (ed.), *Advocates of Reform: From Wyclif to Erasmus,* Library of Christian Classics, vol. 14. London: SCM, 1953: pp. 295–379.

Flood, John L. 'Martin Luther's Bible Translation in Its German and European Context'. *The Bible in the Renaissance: Essays on Biblical Commentary and Translation in the Fifteenth and Sixteenth Centuries.* Aldershot: Ashgate, 2001: pp. 45–70.

Forde, Gerhard O. *The Captivation of the Will: Luther vs. Erasmus on Freedom and Bondage,* Lutheran Quarterly Books. Grand Rapids and Cambridge: Wm. B. Eerdmans, 2005.

Gerrish, B. A. 'By Faith Alone: Medium and Message in Luther's Gospel'. *The Old Protestantism and the New: Essays on the Reformation Heritage.* Edinburgh: T&T Clark, 1982: pp. 69–89.

Gerrish, B. A. *The Old Protestantism and the New: Essays on the Reformation Heritage.* Edinburgh: T&T Clark, 1982.

Gregory of Nyssa. 'On Pilgrimage'. In P. Schaff and H. Wace (eds), *The Life and Writings of Gregory of Nyssa,* Nicene and Post-Nicene Fathers, 2nd Series, vol. 5. Grand Rapids: Eerdmans, 1892.

Greschat, Martin. *Martin Bucer: A Reformer and His Time,* translated by Stephen E. Buckwalter. Louisville: Westminster John Knox, 2004.

Haemig, M. J. 'Practical Advice on Prayer from Martin Luther'. *Word & World* 35:1 (2015): 22–30.

Hamm, Berndt. *Frömmigkeit Am Anfang Des 16. Jahrhunderts: Studien Zu Johannes Von Paltz Und Seinem Umkreis*. Tübingen: Mohr, 1982.

Härle, Wilfried. 'Rethinking Paul and Luther'. *Lutheran Quarterly* 20:3 (2006): 303–17.

Hendrix, S. H. *Luther and the Papacy: Stages in a Reformation Conflict*. Philadelphia: Fortress Press, 1981.

Hendrix, S. H. 'Luther on Marriage'. In Timothy J. Wengert (ed.), *Harvesting Martin Luther's Reflections on Theology, Ethics, and the Church*. Grand Rapids and Cambridge: Wm. B. Eerdmans, 1984: pp. 169–84.

Hinlicky, Paul R. *Luther and the Beloved Community: A Path for Christian Theology after Christendom*. Grand Rapids: Eerdmans, 2010.

Hus, Jan. 'On Simony'. In M. Spinka (ed.), *Advocates of Reform: From Wyclif to Erasmus*, Library of Christian Classics, vol. 14. London: SCM, 1953: pp. 196–278.

Iserloh, E. *The Theses Were Not Posted*. London: Geoffrey Chapman, 1968.

Janz, Denis R. *Luther on Thomas Aquinas: The Angelic Doctor in the Thought of the Reformer*. Wiesbaden: Franz Steiner, 1989.

Jenson, Robert W. 'An Ontology of Freedom in the *De Servo Arbitrio* of Luther'. *Modern Theology* 10:3 (1994): 247–52.

Kantzenbach, Friedrich. 'Luthers Sprache Der Bible'. In Hans Volz (ed.), *Martin Luthers Deutsch Bibel*. Hamburg: Friedrich Wittig Verlag, 1978: pp. 7–18.

Karant-Nunn, Susan C. 'Reformation Society, Women and the Family'. In Andrew Pettegree (ed.), *The Reformation World*. London: Routledge, 2000: pp. 433–60.

Kleineidam, Erich. 'Ursprung Und Gegenstand Der Theologie Bei Bernhard Von Clairvaux Und Martin Luther'. In Ernst Wilhelm, Feiereis Konrad and Fritz Hoffmann (eds), *Dienst Der Vermittlung: Festschrift Zum 25-Jährigen Bestehen Des Philosophisch-Theologischen Studiums Im Priesterseminar Erfurt*, Erfurter Theologische Studien. Leipzig: St. Benno-Verlag, 1977: pp. 221–47.

Lehmann, Martin E. *Luther and Prayer*. Milwaukee: Northwestern, 1985.

Lohse, Bernard. *Martin Luther's Theology: Its Historical and Systematic Development*. Minneapolis: Fortress Press, 1999.

Lortz, Joseph. *Die Refomation in Deutschland*, 4th edn. Freiburg: Herder, 1982.

Luther, Martin. *D. Martin Luthers Werke: Kritische Gesamtausgabe*, 73 vols. Weimar: Böhlau, 1883.

Luther, Martin. *Luther's Works*, 55 vols. St Louis and Philadelphia: Concordia and Fortress Press, 1955.

Marius, Richard. *Martin Luther: The Christian between God and Death*. Cambridge, MA: Harvard University Press, 1999.

Matheson, Peter. 'Angels, Depression and "The Stone": A Late Medieval Prayer Book'. *JTS* 48 (1997): 517–30.

Matsuura, Jun. 'Restbestände Aus Der Bibliothek Des Erfurter Augustinerklosters Zu Luthers Zeit Und Bisher Unbekannte Eigenhändige Notizen Luthers: Ein Berichte'. *Lutheriana: Zum 500. Geburtstag Martin Luthers Von Den Mitarbeitern Der Weimarer Ausgabe,* Archiv zur Weimarer Ausgabe der Werke Martin Luthers, vol. 5. Köln: Böhlau, 1984: pp. 315–32.

McGrath, Alister. *In the Beginning: The Story of the King James Bible and How It Changed a Nation, a Language and a Culture.* New York: Doubleday, 2001.

McGrath, Alister. *Luther's Theology of the Cross.* Oxford: Blackwell, 1985.

McGrath, Alister. *Iustitia Dei: A History of the Christian Doctrine of Justification.* Cambridge: Cambridge Universty Press, 1998.

Nicol, Martin. *Meditation Bei Luther,* Forschungen zur Kirchen- und Dogmengeschichte, vol. 34. Göttingen: Vandenhoeck & Ruprecht, 1984.

Nicolson, Adam. *When God Spoke English: The Making of the King James Bible.* London: Harper, 2011.

Norton, David. *A History of the Bible as Literature.* Cambridge: Cambridge University Press, 1993.

Oberman, Heiko A. *Luther: Man between God and the Devil.* New Haven: Yale, 1989.

Oberman, Heiko A. *The Harvest of Medieval Theology: Gabriel Biel and Late Medieval Nominalism.* Cambridge, MA: Harvard University Press, 1963.

Oberman, Heiko A. *Luther: Mensch Zwischen Gott Und Teufel.* Berlin: Severin und Siedler, 1981.

Oberman, Heiko A. *The Reformation: Roots and Ramifications,* translated by Andrew Colin Gow. Edinburgh: T&T Clark, 1994.

Piper, John. *The Future of Justification: A Response to N. T. Wright.* Wheaton: Crossway, 2006.

Posset, Franz. 'Monastic Influence on Martin Luther'. *Monastic Studies* 18 (1988): 136–63.

Posset, Franz. 'Recommendation by Martin Luther on Saint Bernard's *On Consideration'. Cistercian Studies* 25:1 (1990): 25–36.

Ricoeur, Paul. *On Translation, Thinking in Action.* London: Routledge, 2006.

Rogers, M. '"Deliver Us from the Evil One": Martin Luther on Prayer'. *Themelios* 34:3 (2009): 335–47.

Roper, Lyndal. *Martin Luther: Renegade and Prophet.* London: Bodley Head, 2016.

Ryrie, Alec. *Being Protestant in Reformation Britain*. Oxford: Oxford University Press, 2013.

Sanders, E. P. *Paul and Palestinian Judaism*. London: SCM, 1977.

Sanders, E. P. *Paul*. New York: Oxford University Press, 1991.

Schwarz, Reinhard. 'Luther's Inalienable Inheritance of Monastic Theology'. *American Benedictine Review* 39 (1988): 430–50.

Scwarz, Hans. *True Faith in the True God: An Introduction to Luther's Life and Thought*. Minneapolis: Augsburg, 1996.

Seifrid, Mark A. 'Luther, Melanchthon and Paul on the Question of Imputation'. In Mark Husbands and Daniel J. Treier (eds), *Justification: What's at Stake in the Current Debates*. Downers Grove: Intervarsity Press, 2004: pp. 137–52.

Smith, James K. A. *Desiring the Kingdom: Worship, Worldview and Cultural Formation*. Grand Rapids: Baker Academic, 2009.

Steinmetz, David C. *Luther in Context*, 2nd edn. Grand Rapids: Baker Academic, 2002.

Stendahl, Krister. *Paul among Jews and Gentiles*. Philadelphia: Fortress Press, 1976.

Tauler, Johannes. *Sermons*. New Jersey: Paulist Press, 1985.

Theodore G. Tappert (trans. and ed.). *The Book of Concord: The Confessions of the Evangelical Lutheran Church*. Philadelphia: Fortress Press, 1959.

Tomlin, Graham. *The Power of the Cross: Theology and the Death of Christ in Paul, Luther and Pascal*. Carlisle: Paternoster, 1999.

Twain, Mark. *The Innocents Abroad, or the New Pilgrim's Progress*. Hartford, CT: American, 1869.

Von Loewenich, Walter. *Luther's Theology of the Cross*. Belfast: Christian Journals, 1976.

Watson, Philip S. *Let God be God! An Interpretation of the Theology of Martin Luther*. London: Epworth, 1947.

Wengert, Timothy J. *Law and Gospel: Philip Melanchthon's Debate with John Agricola of Eisleben over* Poenitentia. Grand Rapids: Baker, 1997.

Westerholm, Stephen. *Perspectives Old and New on Paul: The 'Lutheran' Paul and His Critics*. Grand Rapids: Eerdmans, 2004.

Wright, N. T. *Paul: Fresh Perspectives*. London: SPCK, 2005.

Wright, N. T. *Justification: God's Plan and Paul's Vision*. London: SPCK, 2009.

Yeago, David S. 'The Catholic Luther'. In Carl E. Braaten and Robert W. Jenson (eds), *The Catholicity of the Reformation*. Grand Rapids and Cambridge: Wm. B. Eerdmans, 1996: pp. 13–34.

NAME INDEX

GENERAL INDEX